Information Centre
Xerox
Bessemer Road
WELWYN GARDEN CITY
Herts. AL7 1HE

WINNING PRESENTATIONS

Winning *presentations*

David Gilgrist
with Rex Davies

Gower

Published by
Gower Publishing Limited
Gower House
Croft Road
Aldershot
Hampshire GU11 3HR
England

Gower
Old Post Road
Brookfield
Vermont 05036
USA

British Library Cataloguing in Publication Data
Gilgrist, David
  Winning presentations
  1.Business presentations
  I.Title II.Davies, Rex
  658.4'5

ISBN 0 566 07717 5

Library of Congress Cataloging-in-Publication Data
Gilgrist, David
  Winning presentations / David Gilgrist with Rex Davies.
    p. cm.
  ISBN 0-566-07717-5 (hardback)
  1. Business presentations—Handbooks, manuals, etc. I. Davies, Rex, 1955– . II. Title.
HF5718.22.G55 1996
658.4'52—dc20   96-901
                                                                    CIP

Typeset in Palatino/Avant Garde by Photoprint, Torquay and printed in Great Britain at the University Press, Cambridge.

Contents

List of figures   ix

How to use this book   xi

Preface   xiii

Fast Track

1   **The effective presentation**   1
    The format   3
    The one-way part – the formal delivery of
    your presentation   5
    The two-way part – the interactive question-
    and-answer or discussion period   7

2   **Analysing your audience**   9
    The three key questions   11
                            Why analyse your audience?   117
                            How to analyse your audience   118

3   **Strategies for success**   17
    Define your objective   19
                            Two alternative strategies   119
    Persuasive strategy   19
                            Stating your action up-front   120
                            Validation of the strategy   123

Contents

	Using the persuasive approach	124
	Informative/educational strategy	23
	Using the informative/educational approach	125
	Need to know or need to act?	126
4	**Preparing your presentation**	27
	The anatomy of a presentation	29
	Why a method approach?	127
	The overview	29
	The overview – off to a flying start	127
	The body – the sub-topics	39
	The body – fleshing out your sub-topics	133
	The final summary	55
	The summary – the final message	141
	The importance of a balanced presentation	142
	How to ensure a balanced presentation	145
5	**Delivering your message**	59
	Positioning	61
	Sight lines and scanning	63
	Voice	67
	Mannerisms and dress	71
	The non-verbal aspects of presenting	147
	The objective of the non-verbal method	155
6	**Designing and using visual aids**	77
	The formats	81
	Which visual aids to choose	156
	Formatting your visual aids	157
	Operating the overhead projector	91
7	**Handling questions**	95
	Planning the question-and-answer session	97
	The importance of the question-and-answer-session	161
	The question-handling strategy	99
	Strategies for handling questions	163
	Identifying and closing the gap	101
	How to assess if your answer has closed the gap	164
	Using the question-and-answer technique	167
	Problems with questions	105

Additional techniques   167
Concluding the question-and-answer session   109
The all-important summary   169

Winning Presentations checklist   111

Supplementary information and examples   115
See italic listings above

List of figures

2.1   Audience analysis form   15
4.1   Overview planner   37
4.2   Sub-topic message planner   53
4.3   Summary planner   57
6.1   Textual visual aid format   87
6.2   Graphical visual aid format   89

How to use this book

This book is based on the assumption that you have a presentation to give, and soon. Therefore you do not have time to study its contents in full. What you need is a proven method of persuasive communication that can be quickly applied to good effect.

This is it.

Sections of this book have been extracted and assembled to provide a 'fast track'. Follow these sections at the beginning of the book. They will enable you to quickly design and competently deliver an effective presentation.

When you have been successful you may wish to explore the thinking behind the method. The remaining sections of the book contain detailed supporting material which is cross-referenced to the fast track and designed to further enhance your abilities.

Preface

About the Learning Point Presentations School   xv
Background to the School's method   xvi

Preface

About the Learning Point Presentations School

The Learning Point Presentations School is a dedicated organization that works predominantly with firms in the City of London and internationally with the top banks, insurance companies, accountants, consultants, law firms, property organizations and service sector corporates to provide presentation techniques training and associated consultancy support. Companies use the school to achieve better conversion rates or improve reactions and outcomes in their 'beauty parades', client seminars, review meetings and AGMs. Internal departments such as IT, Quality and Compliance use the School's methods for persuasive communication in the process of managing change. The School is now in its sixteenth year and its success is due, in no small part, to its rigorous and continuing research into identifying the factors that make for a winning presentation. The resulting methodology does not simply encompass conventional public speaking techniques, but is instead an approach for the construction and delivery of presentations that is effective in both individual and team situations.

This book is a comprehensive, step-by-step guide to the preparation and delivery of a winning presentation. We particularly intend it as a quick and effective 'how-to' guide for business people presenting at pitches, product launches and AGMs where the outcome is critical. It is for these readers that the unique feature of the title is intended – a 'fast track' component to the book outlining the principal aspects of composition, delivery, teamwork and question-handling techniques. These sections are provided for quick reference for people in a hurry.

Using a combination of diagrams and minimal text, our method will enable you to make significant improvements to your presentations in a very short time. Once the method is proven, you will naturally be encouraged to study the remainder of the book with its detailed supporting material designed to further enhance your abilities.

Background to the School's method

In the early 1980s my work in developing marketing programmes and training responses was often conducted in conjunction with researchers undertaking analysis to identify the factors that made winners so successful. Focusing on the activities that distinguished successful presenters produced a common formula for the construction of their messages and content. Building on these initial findings on content, I extended the analysis to understand the audience expectations. My research looked at the audiences of pension fund trustees, intermediaries, AGMs, roadshows and finance and policy committee meetings. Their responses indicated a number of needs and preferences.

First, and above all, audiences want their presenters to be blessed with a daunting array of *intangible qualities*. They expect their potential providers to be personable, able to articulate strategy with wit as well as clarity and display ample amounts of confidence. In addition to all this, audiences expect presenters to have the technical expertise to get the job done, beat the market or interpret complex legal issues.

Being invited to pitch for business is analogous to a

selection interview. It is usually the culmination of a written selection process – a questionnaire has been completed or a tender document has been submitted at which stage the rational qualifications such as track record, technical expertise, have been assessed. Once you reach the oral stage, then all those rational criteria for selection will have been approved and clients are now asking themselves 'Do we see eye to eye with these people? Do they share our view of the world? Is the confidence there? Is the chemistry right?' These are such subjective, intangible areas that we have seen companies with excellent credentials on paper lose the business through an indifferent presentation, whilst their unpromising competitors went on to win purely on the strength of their oral presentation. Many organizations will present their product, service differentiators or track record, but in a service industry or profession, such as law, these differentiators are harder to identify. In these circumstances it is the individual presenter who is the differentiator, and success will depend on that person's ability to generate those intangible qualities and confidence, or at the very least not provide an obvious reason to be eliminated.

Second, many who work in the professions, and more generally in business and commerce, are not typically 'front-of-house' types. Though expert in their own field, these people may be more used to interacting with computer screens and documents than demonstrating their worth to potential clients. To solve this dilemma many companies bring out their most persuasive presenter – the 'silver-tongued front person' – the senior partner, director or marketing executive. This approach carries a serious risk since, if audiences or potential clients detect this, they can react quite negatively. They want to see and feel confident about the person who will be doing the job. Many invitations from potential clients now stipulate that they wish to see the people who will be doing the work or undertaking the project. If clients suspect a front, then during the question-and-answer session they will question the presenter intensively, probing for weaknesses in their knowledge. Whilst many of the marketing professionals we have worked with have a broad understanding of the products and services offered by their companies, many lack the detailed knowledge of the specifics rendering them vulnerable to in-depth questioning. We have had notable success in using our methods to train analysts, fund managers, lawyers and technical specialists to communicate their expertise confidently and effectively and, by dispensing with the 'silver-tongue', win business in their own right.

Most presentations are won or lost in the question-and-answer session. This is where clients and shareholders assess *ability under stress*. If you cannot handle difficult questions with confidence then they will infer that you are not confident in your job and they will be similarly hesitant in investing their money with you, accepting your interpretation of corporate law or believing your ability to manage the company. In fact there is no correlation between reacting quickly and confidently to the stressful demands of your job and your ability to give a good answer to a probing question following a presentation, but clients tend to make this inference. Being unable to give a satisfactory explanation to shareholders about directors' remuneration does not in itself indicate inability to run the company. But shareholders may well make that connection.

Finally, you may be involved in a team presentation – a joint pitch where a number of specialists come together (often for the first time) to present. The potential for a ramshackle performance is enormous, and audiences detect the lack of coordination, reporting that many of these so-called teams seem to have 'met in the taxi for the first time on the way over'. There are techniques and rules for team presentations that can produce a cohesive performance and a significant improvement in results.

Many books have been written about presentation skills. They contain tips and techniques that are thought to be effective but are not necessarily proven in the hard-headed world of winning business. This book contains validated methods and formulae, tried and tested with clients and audiences in some of the most fiercely competitive markets in the world.

Validate it for yourself.

David Gilgrist

Chapter 1

The effective presentation

The format   3
The one-way part – the formal delivery of
your presentation   5
The two-way part – the interactive
question-and-answer or discussion period   7

1

1   THE EFFECTIVE PRESENTATION

The format

Effective presentations comprise two distinct parts: the formal (one-way) presentation followed by a (two-way) question-and-answer session.

The formal part should not be more than 15 minutes long, even if you are presenting as a team. Using more than one presenter enables you to hold the audience for a little longer, but the average (passive) adult attention span is about 13 minutes that average is reducing year on year.

You should allow up to three times the one-way period for the question-and-answer session.

Keep the two parts distinct. Avoid questions during the formal presentation, or you risk carrying out neither part successfully.

The one-way part – the formal delivery of your presentation

Audiences cannot take in very much fact and detail, so aim to communicate simplified messages, up to a *maximum* of three.

To convey your messages you will need to perform competently in three areas simultaneously:

- **Non-verbal**: traditional public-speaking techniques. These comprise how you stand, how you speak, what to do with your hands and eye contact.
- **Verbal**: the actual content of your presentation. The Learning Point Presentations School formula and strategies can be used to construct effective messages and obtain objective feedback.
- **Visual**: computer screens, acetates, slides and paper-based accompaniments to your presentation. The design format developed by the Learning Point Presentations School will not only enable

your audience to see what you are saying as they hear you say it, it will also enable you to dispense with notes and cue-cards so that you can focus your delivery on the audience.

The two-way part – the interactive question-and-answer or discussion period

Your mission here is to dispel any negative evaluation of your messages resulting from the one-way part, maintain your initiative and not allow your messages to be sidetracked or sidelined. We call this 'crowd control'. Most presentations are won or lost at this stage. Do not leave it to chance. Preparing for this session is even more important than work on the formal presentation.

Chapter 2

Analysing your audience

The three key questions   11
                  Why analyse your audience?   117
               How to analyse your audience   118

2   ANALYSING YOUR AUDIENCE

The three key questions

Your audience is the first thing you
need to consider. Answer these
three questions, using the audience
analysis form shown in Figure 2.1 to
record this information.

What do you know about the audience?

Who they are, what they do and
their experiences in doing it are all
factors that will inform your
presentation. Do some detective
work, talk to people who know
them or simply telephone them
and ask! Make an educated guess
about anything you are unsure of.

What are their parochial interests?

What is their current situation? What
are the issues that concern them –
the problems they must solve, the
questions to which they want
answers?
   Remember, this question

concerns not only the audience's interest in your subject, it also includes their interests *per se*.

What is your objective?

Understanding your audience will help you to set an objective that meets *their* needs. See 'Strategies for success' (page 17) for further information.

Audience Analysis

What do you know about the audience?

What are their parochial interests?

Your objective
  to inform them about
  and/or
  to persuade them to

Figure 2.1 *Audience analysis form*

Chapter 3

Strategies for success

Define your objective	19
Two alternative strategies	119
Persuasive strategy	19
Stating your action up-front	120
Validation of the strategy	123
Using the persuasive approach	124
Informative/educational strategy	23
Using the informative/educational approach	125
Need to know or need to act?	126

3   STRATEGIES FOR SUCCESS

Define your objective

Is your presentation designed to:

1   persuade your audience to commit to a course of action

or

2   inform and educate them on a particular subject?

Depending on your intention there are two distinct strategies.

Persuasive strategy

Your objective is for your audience to understand enough to approve the decision to buy into what you propose. You must ensure that your main argument is not weakened by peripheral detail. Your persuasive presentation will succeed only if you avoid argument dilution and use the decision as the anchor point and focus of the presentation.

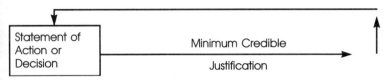

Decide the minimum credible justification – the least amount of argument that you can credibly give – without leaving the audience dissatisfied. Arrange the points of your case in sequence: the strongest point first, weakest next, second strongest last – the 1-3-2 rule (see page 125 for a detailed explanation).

Prepare potential questions. Brainstorm the questions that, by keeping your justification to a minimum, you have left unanswered. Also note the questions that a rehearsal stimulates and make sure you can answer them (see page 163 for a detailed explanation).

21

Informative/educational strategy

Full understanding of your subject by the audience is your objective here. All aspects of the matter can be disclosed. However, in your logical argument, you should consider the relative size of each learning step by reference to the audience's knowledge or expertise.

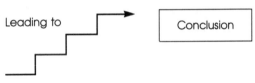

Logical Argument

Expect to handle interventions and questions as you go through each step. This is the audience's route to achieving full understanding.

Remember, an informative situation demands a 'need to know' message and you want your audience to understand the subject fully. A persuasive situation demands a 'need to act' message and you only want your audience to understand enough to act. **Note the difference between the two strategies. In the**

23

informative approach the presenter makes the case for. In the persuasive strategy, the audience has to make the case against – unaided!

Chapter 4

Preparing your presentation

The anatomy of a presentation   29
                          Why a method approach?   127
The overview   29
                 The overview – off to a flying start   127
The body – the sub-topics   39
            The body – fleshing out your sub-topics   133
The final summary   55
                    The summary – the final message   141
        The importance of a balanced presentation   142
        How to ensure a balanced presentation   145

4   PREPARING YOUR PRESENTATION

The anatomy of a presentation

There are three main sections to a presentation

- the overview
- the body
- the summary.

The overview

As an introduction to your presentation, the overview is important for two reasons. First, the opening is the time of maximum scrutiny by your audience who are waiting to hear what you have to say. Second, the overview is the 'blueprint' of your presentation, and any flaws it contains will emerge as flaws in the presentation. So both its design and delivery are critical to the success of the presentation as a whole.

Get it right by including the following:

- **The purpose**: a clear statement of what the presentation will do for your audience, either
  - 'give you an insight into/ understanding of/ appreciation of' when your purpose is to inform and educate, or
  - 'seek your approval/win your mandate/gain your commitment (to a certain course of action)' when persuasion is your aim.
  Avoid vague terms such as 'look at', 'talk about' or 'examine' which are processes, not purposes.
- **The map**: an agenda of the one, two or maximum three sub-topic headings that you will cover. Each sub-topic will have a key point or message, and three messages are the maximum that your audience can be relied upon to take in.
- **The gain or hook**: to make

your audience want to listen
to you. Choose from
- *opportunity*: the benefits
  that your audience can
  obtain by listening
- *enhanced opportunity*: as
  above but using an
  analogy to which your
  audience can relate, so
  presenting a more familiar
  or simpler picture of a
  more complex opportunity
- *fear or threat*: the
  consequences or
  penalties of their not
  listening
- *decision criteria*: a
  demonstrated
  understanding of the
  decision that your
  audience have to make
  or the questions to which
  they need answers
- *mystery*: a statement that
  arouses your audience's
  curiosity, followed by the
  promise that all will be
  revealed
- *showstopper*: a (relevant)
  startling statement or
  powerful rhetorical

question that will seize
their attention.

If you use this formula, your
audience will know where they are
going (*purpose*), how they'll get
there (*map*), and why they should
be going (*gain/hook*).

Plan your overview using the
format given overleaf in Figure 4.1.

Rehearse your overview as
thoroughly as time permits.
**Remember: there is no second
chance to make a first
impression**.

Overview

Content

Purpose (What will this presentation do?)

Map (Sub-topics and messages or decision criteria questions)

-

-

-

Gain (Why should they listen to it? or the penalty for not listening)

Figure 4.1 *Overview planner*

The body – the sub-topics

If your intention is to persuade, your sub-topics should be presented strongest first, second strongest last and weakest (if there is a third) in the middle.

For the informative, educational approach, arrange the sub-topics in a step-by-step sequence ranging from the simplest to the most difficult.

To ensure that it is effective, construct each sub-topic in your presentation to a certain formula. Each needs an *equal mix* of information, elaboration, integration and emphasis.

- **Inform** your audience with facts, views, ideas or opinions.
- Give examples, analogies, anecdotes and research findings to **elaborate** upon, and prove, these views and opinions.
- Use **integration** to involve your audience and to relate your material to their own experiences and situation.
- Give **emphasis** so that the audience takes notice of, and remembers, points you want to make.

Aim for 25 per cent in each category.

The message – what you want your audience to remember and the information you need to do it

Decide the message of each sub-topic. (If you are using the decision criteria approach then each sub-topic will answer one of your audience's key questions.)

Don't succumb to the temptation to include large amounts of information – be selective and use the minimum number of facts, views and opinions needed to convey your message. Make statements that you can prove and that your audience can relate to.

Identify the appropriate facts, either:

- the minimum you judge necessary to take your audience through a particular step on their way to full understanding of a subject (when your objective is to **inform** and **educate**), or
- the minimum to answer credibly a question in the audience's mind or justify your action (where your objective is to **persuade**).

Use **numbering** and **labels** to break the information down into smaller, more easily identifiable and assimilated pieces – for example, 'The three (*numbering*) key (*labelling*) aspects of this sub-topic are ...'. You can also label what you intend to say next – for example, 'So in conclusion ...', 'To summarize, then ...'.

Too many facts will bore your audience. Too few will make your presentation seem superficial.

Elaboration – helping your audience see what you mean (seeing is believing)

When people say 'I hear what you're saying ...', they are usually disagreeing. However, when they say 'I see what you mean ...', they have taken your point. That is the purpose of elaboration.

Make your statements more powerful, more educational and more convincing by using:

- **Examples or analogies**. Illustrate by direct examples that are tangible and pitched at a level suited to the audience. Use analogies to help non-technical

audiences understand complex concepts – specialists in the audience will appreciate their novelty.

- **Drawings, photos, graphs, pie-charts, histograms etc**. Make use of anything that you can show your audience in visual form.
- **Third party references**. Independent research findings and endorsements from other clients, if credible and relevant to your audience, are a good source of proof.
- **Anecdotes**. As an expert in the subject of your talk, your experiences and anecdotal evidence will also show audiences what you mean.

Too much elaboration, however, will make you sound like a boring 'little professor'. Too little and your presentation will simply not be credible. Match your elaboration to the facts that support your message.

Integration – relating what you say to your audience

Integration has two functions: relating parts of your presentation to each other; and, more

importantly, relating your material
to the audience. Integrate by:

- **relating to your audience's experiences**, identifying things they will have seen and done, aspects they have in common and collective experiences. Relate your examples or other elaboration directly to these. If there is little commonality of experience amongst your audience, use everyday experiences or current affairs.

- **relating to your audience's situation** by showing how your presentation content can affect the audience in their job, career, social or domestic situation. Demonstrate the relationship between your presentation and their world. This is a natural sales behaviour so be careful not to overdo it.

Without integration, your presentation may be seen as irrelevant. Avoid audience reactions of 'So what?' and 'What's this got to do with me?' by relating your material directly to them.

Emphasis – ensuring that your audience retains the message

Audiences can only cope with a limited number of messages. Ensure that the message of each sub-topic is absorbed by:

- **stating importance** using words such as 'key', 'critical', 'crucial', 'vital', 'significant' and 'important' before a point to seize the attention of your audience.
- **summarizing** after every key point and the message at the end of each sub-topic. A powerful way to make summary points easier to recall is by using a 'soundbite' – a concise memorable phrase, slogan or metaphor.
- **using rhetorical questions and pauses**. 'Just think for a moment ...', 'Ask yourself ...', 'Imagine the consequences of ...', and 'Consider the effect of ...' are all ways of prefacing your rhetorical questions so that you will not have to deal with an answer.

49

Your audience will work with your material in the pause following your question, and if they work with it they are more likely to remember it.

- **using humour and asides**. A favourite with any audience, humour is memorable and thus a powerful vehicle for emphasis. However, random humour can obscure your point. Avoid this by linking the humour to your message.

Without emphasis your audience will pick up a random and probably incorrect message from your sub-topic. Using the verbal techniques listed above will ensure that the audience retains the messages that you want them to.

Plan your sub-topics using the format shown in Figure 4.2.

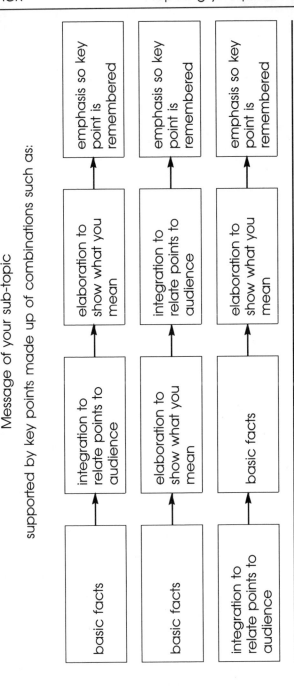

Figure 4.2 *Sub-topic message planner*

The final summary

To be effective this summary should:

- **repeat the principal messages** from each of the sub-topics which will link in with and enable you to
- **deliver the 'signature' or one key message**. This should refer back to the **gain** or **hook** used in the overview and complete the presentation.

Since audiences retain best the first and last things they hear, the summary, like the opening overview, is a time of heightened audience attention. Rehearse your summary thoroughly for maximum effect.

Plan your summary using the format shown in Figure 4.3.

Remember

- Overview to grab attention and 'set out stall'.
- The body with a balance of informing, elaborating, integrating and emphasizing.
- The final summary containing key messages and the signature.

Summary

Content

Message of Sub-topic 1

Message of Sub-topic 2

Message of Sub-topic 3

Main message
(Signature)

Figure 4.3 *Summary planner*

Chapter 5

Delivering your message

Positioning   61
Sight lines and scanning   63
Voice   67
Mannerisms and dress   71
   The non-verbal aspects of presenting   147
   The objective of the non-verbal method   155

5   DELIVERING YOUR MESSAGE

The many tips and techniques which you can use to perfect your delivery style can be grouped into four areas:

- positioning
- sight lines and scanning
- voice and delivery
- mannerisms and dress.

Positioning

When giving larger, more formal presentations you are unlikely to inspire an audience if you remain motionless and only visible from above chest height. So avoid standing behind a lectern – come out in front or stand to the side. Ensure that any microphone provided can still pick you up and, if using a clip-mike, remember to remove it before you leave the stage.

With smaller groups resist the temptation to sit down behind a desk. You will be at the same eye

level as your audience and will be
less able to exert the influence and
control you would have from a
standing position. Also, your ability
to move and breathe properly will
be more restricted and your
delivery may suffer.

Wherever possible stand and
deliver, and share this delivery with
all parts of the audience. In a
small room address them all by
gesture or shift of weight; in a
larger room move around the
stage to reach the extreme wings.

Make sure you are in a position
to move and address all of your
audience.

Sight lines and scanning

The principle here is to see and be
seen. A common arrangement in
business presentations is the 'U'
shape, with the audience seated
around three sides of the room.
Avoid the temptation to move
forward and address the back of
the 'U', to the exclusion of those at
the sides. Stand back so that you
can see everyone without the
deliberate effort of turning.

Avoid presenting with your back

to a window or strong light source
because:

- it will tire your audience and
  you will appear only in
  silhouette, unable to make
  eye contact with them
- there may be more
  interesting distractions behind
  you
- particularly for women
  presenters the 'see-through'
  effect on lightweight clothing
  can be distracting.

Do not focus all your attention on
the one friendly face in the
audience – you will embarrass
them and alienate their
colleagues. Nor should you focus
on the individual whom you judge
most powerful – they may not be.
Speak to *all* of the audience. If eye
contact is uncomfortable for you
focus on the area of forehead
immediately above the bridge of
the nose. This gives the impression
of eye contact without the
discomfort or risk of 'locking on' to
one person.

In some parts of your audience
visual aid equipment can obscure
you or the image it is presenting.

You may obscure the image yourself if you don't stand away to the side. Avoid both pitfalls and ensure that your audience have a clear sight of both you and your visuals. Always try to maintain a triangular arrangement between you, the visual image and your audience.

Visual contact with your audience is the aim here.

Voice

To present clearly and audibly you need to breathe correctly. This will enable you to generate volume and resonance from the diaphragm and chest. Breathe in by pushing your stomach out which pulls your diaphragm down, expanding your rib-cage and filling your lungs with air. Control your voice by tightening your stomach muscles as you exhale to give extra clarity and audiblity. Pace yourself slower than normal conversation speed. Your delivery should sound rather slow and deliberate – to you. Normal speed is too fast for your audience to take everything in. It may be useful to imagine you are

speaking to a roomful of people whose first language is not English. Speaking more slowly will make you sound more authoritative, especially on the key points and messages of your presentation.

Modulate your voice to give it a rhythmic and listenable quality. Avoid a monotone delivery in which everything you say sounds the same. If your voice lacks variety, write out your presentation in full and mark those words where you wish to change the tone of your voice. Raising your pitch on key words can make you sound more positive. Adopt the television presenter technique of stressing every third or fifth word or syllable to import a rhythmic quality to your voice.

Your delivery will be significantly enhanced by using pauses for effect, to give emphasis and add weight and balance. The problem is that a pause which seems like an eternity to you will hardly register with your audience. Achieve the right length by counting to five (in your head).

Remember, your voice is the instrument on which you play the

content of your presentation. Do it
justice.

Mannerisms and dress

The objective here is to project
your own personality. Don't put on
an act. If your audience are fooled
by the act they are buying a
deception and will be
subsequently disappointed.
Conversely, if they dislike your act
they have a reason to reject what
you are saying. Be authentic.

Exotic accessories are pendulous
earrings, bow-ties, heavily
patterned ties, buttonholes and
brooches – anything that takes the
audience's eyes away from your
face. Even if they are part of your
everyday style and a personal
statement, remove them. Don't
force your message to compete
with other visual 'statements'.

Use your hands for dramatic
effect – for illustration, for emphasis
and to generate movement and
energy. When they are not being
used in these purposeful ways,
adopt the 'home' position – loosely
together, slightly above the belt
line. Practise this; it may feel slightly

uncomfortable at first but other positions look awkward and uncomfortable and can send inappropriate signals to your audience. Again, watch television presenters and weather forecasters to see how they use their hands or keep them at rest.

Excessive 'um's and 'er's can be a problem. Similarly, peculiar idiosyncratic mannerisms can be distracting and irritating to an audience. Repetition of particular words or phrases is another example of these subconscious actions which presenters use to fill the silence or overcome embarrassment. Ask your colleagues for feedback on these – awareness of these problems is the first step to resolving them.

Remember, look (and act) the part.

Remember that **the key to delivery is to make and maintain contact with your audience**, which is the purpose of these non-verbal behaviours.

- **Position** yourself so that you can move and project.

- Maintain visual contact, see and be seen by ensuring that your **sight lines** are clear.
- Make it easy for your audience to listen to you with a clear, well modulated **voice**.
- Look and act the part and reduce any distractions caused by your **mannerisms or dress**.

Chapter 6

Designing and using visual aids

The formats   81
                    Which visual aids to choose   156
                    Formatting your visual aids   157
Operating the overhead projector   91

77

6 DESIGNING AND USING VISUAL AIDS

As stated earlier, your principal objective in presentation delivery is contact with your audience. This is harder to achieve if you have continual recourse to notes and cue-cards. Visuals serve a dual purpose: they provide you with cues and prompts, so that you can dispense with notes; and they convey your message to the audience visually. Make sure that *all* your audience can see both you and your visuals clearly.

Choice of medium depends primarily on audience size and the room in which you are presenting. Whether you use an A4 desk-top presenter for a one-on-one session or with a group of three or four, an overhead projector with an audience of a dozen or more or address a large audience using computer graphics or 35mm slides, there are two design formats – one for text visuals, one for graphics –

that work effectively for both audience and presenter.

Design your visuals according to these formats, ensuring that they work for you and enable you to deliver your presentation without any other prompts. If the visuals don't work for you, they are unlikely to work for your audience.

The formats

Each of your visuals needs:

- a **title** to give identity and clearly indicate to the audience what the slide is about
- **bullets, letters or numbers** to separate each point you will make
- text in **upper and lower case**, never capitals because that makes it more difficult to read
- **sparing use of colour**, avoiding the use of red for text (it recedes rather than stands out) and never using red and green together in graphics (difficult for viewers who are colour blind)

- a **maximum of six lines** containing no more than six key words each (the '6 × 6 rule' – see page 159)
- a **strap line** which delivers the main message (see page 159).

A sample of both text and graphic visual aid formats appears in Figures 6.1 and 6.2. Note that the inclusion of graphics does not change the need for text. Regardless of the type of graphic you use – photograph, drawing, pie-chart or histogram – reduce it in scale and complexity. There will always be sufficient visualization to illustrate the design, the trend or comparison you wish to show. This leaves space for your cues which act as a discipline and a prompt for you and also explain to your audience exactly what the visual is saying.

Each image should provide you with between one and a half and two minutes of delivery time. Less than this and your presentation will look like a series of slide changes and be too much for your audience to take in. Spend more

time with each and the visual
impact will start to decay.

Using these visual formats will
give you your cues and prompts
about what to say, whilst
simultaneously conveying your
message to your audience visually.

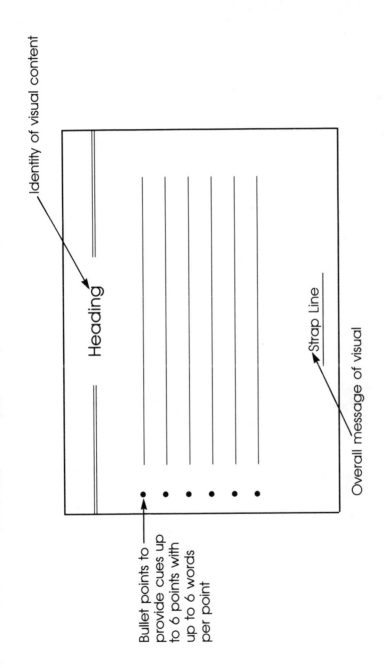

Identity of visual content

Heading

Strap Line

Overall message of visual

Bullet points to
provide cues up
to 6 points with
up to 6 words
per point

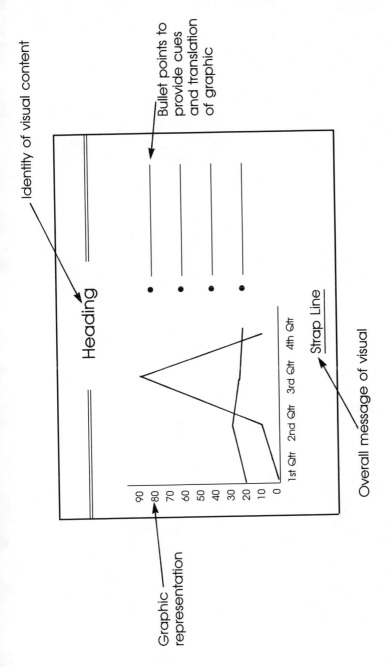

Figure 6.2 *Graphical visual aid format*

Operating the overhead projector

The overhead projector is one of the most versatile of all visual aids. Ensure that you use it in the most effective way by employing the following sequence. Having positioned your first slide and introduced it to relax the audience, then:

- Switch on and stand to the side.
- Allow time for the audience to digest the image.
- Elaborate on the visual cue points.
- Summarize using the strap line.
- Switch off but do not touch the slide.
- Introduce the next slide to relax the audience.
- Then, and *only then* change the slides over.

Then repeat the sequence from the *switch on* stage.

Adopting this sequence allows you to maintain contact with your audience throughout your presentation. It avoids you talking to the projector or your slides on the table or dazzling your audience with a blank white screen.

Remember, your audience came to see and hear your presentation not watch you struggle with your equipment.

With any visual aid equipment try to avoid using pointers; look for an alternative visual way of highlighting. When using an overhead projector, if there is no alternative to pointing, use a telescopic pointer and point to the slide itself not the image on the screen. Pointing to the screen turns you away from your audience and usually produces two visual pointer images pointing at different parts of the image. Avoid the gradual revealing of your slide: audiences find it irritating and are more intrigued by the surprise underneath the mask than attentive to the point you are talking about!

With modern computer graphics and multimedia applications using LCD tablets and back projection equipment there are many alternatives to the overhead projector. Try experimenting with them – the rewards are tremendous.

Chapter 7

Handling questions

Planning the question-and-answer session 97

The importance of the question-and-answer-session 161

The question-handling strategy 99

Strategies for handling questions 163

Identifying and closing the gap 101

How to assess if your answer has closed the gap 164

Using the question-and-answer technique 167

Problems with questions 105

Additional techniques 167

Concluding the question-and-answer session 109

The all-important summary 169

7   HANDLING QUESTIONS

Planning the question-and-answer session

Most presentations that fail do so because of a poor performance in the question-and-answer session. You need to spend as much time rehearsing your answers to questions as you spend preparing the presentation itself.

Your handling of questions must take into account the two basic requirements of the question-and-answer session:

1   to retain control over the proceedings
2   to identify and close the 'gap' of negative evaluation.

Limit your presentation to about 15 minutes and allow up to three times this period for questions. Limiting your presentation keeps you within an audience's average attention threshold and, more importantly, gives your audience less content to evaluate negatively.

The longer the question-and-answer session, the more time you will have to counter any negative reactions and close the evaluation gap.

Very few questions should come as a surprise. You should be able to predict many of the audience's responses and prepare your answers. (See pages 120–23 for further detail.)

The question-handling strategy

The most effective question-handling strategy is as follows:

1 **Give a short answer** so that there is less for your audience to evaluate and thus generate supplementary questions. It also prevents you going off at a tangent or saying something that you may regret. Most importantly the main answer is usually contained in the first sentence with any futher response seldom providing much added value.

2 **Ask a test-back question**,

designed to elicit a yes/no
response from your
questioners, which will give
you feedback on their
degree of acceptance of
your answer.

3 **If the feedback is clearly
   affirmative**, the negative
   evaluation gap is closed and
   you can confidently move on
   to the next question.

4 **If the feedback is negative**,
   you can now decide whether
   to spend time on another
   attempt to close the gap or
   whether to move on. If you
   decide to persist, supplement
   your original response, testing
   back again until you receive
   confirmation of acceptance.
   Use your judgement as to
   how long to stay on one
   point. (See 'Persistent
   questions', page 168 for
   further details.)

Identifying and closing
the gap

Questions are most often prompted
by a negative evaluation gap.

Identify the specific nature of the gap by listening to the language of the question, answering and then adapting your test-back question accordingly.

A request for more detail or facts reveals an **information gap**. Answer, then test back with: 'Does that answer your question?', 'Is that OK?' or 'Happy with that?'

A request for further clarification reveals a **gap in understanding**. Explain further then test how effective your explanation has been by asking: 'Does that clarify the point?' or 'Can you see that now?'

Questions expressing doubts or concerns indicate a **credibility gap** – your audience does not yet believe what you're saying. Offer more proof, justify your approach further then check to see the effect by asking: 'Does that resolve any doubts or concerns?', 'Does that allay your fears?' or 'Are you convinced?'

Watch out for the **test question** – one to which there is a pass or fail answer and often a policy matter (for example, your company's position on green

issues). Try to establish the questioner's position on the subject first then provide an answer conditioned by their response. You may not be able to satisfy them entirely, but this gives you the chance to lessen the impact of a clinical yes/no, pass/fail answer. Test back with 'Does that seem unreasonable?' or 'Would you share our view?' or 'Can you go along with that?'

Remember, giving a short answer then testing back, ideally using the same language as the questioner, is the best way to close any evaluation gap.

Problems with questions

In addition to the question/answer/ test-back formula, use the following techniques:

- **If there are no questions initially, pose one or two of your own** by saying 'We are sometimes asked ...'. However, there are cultural differences to consider. This technique works well with

Western audiences but
Eastern/oriental audiences
require a different approach
(see page 168).

- **Take persistent questioners
  off-line** by asking the rest of
  the group if they still need
  clarification on this point or if
  they would prefer you to deal
  with it later – off-line. It they
  choose the former option you
  have to continue, but if they
  prefer to move on you will
  have resolved your problem.
  With larger audiences
  employ the same principle of
  using the interests of the
  audience as a whole as the
  excuse for moving on.
- **Never answer 'I don't know'**
  to a question. Use a
  euphemism – 'I don't have
  that information to hand', for
  example – and then give a
  time by which you will
  provide the answer.
- **Devise a game plan for
  team questions**. Decide who
  will answer on each
  particular subject. Let the
  team leader deal with any

exceptions and ask the test-back questions. Never add to a colleague's answer unless invited.

- **Avoid platitudes**, such as 'That's a good/interesting question' or 'I'm glad you asked me that'. The questioner may feel patronized and the audience may feel that you are trying to buy time.

Concluding the question-and-answer session

The most important thing to do after the question-and-answer session is to summarize.

Re-present your last visual and restate your key messages in a brief punchy way.

This second summary will ensure that your audience will not go away remembering only the last question and the answer you gave. Control the lasting impressions of your presentation by summarizing at the end of the question-and-answer session.

Winning Presentations checklist

Audience analysis

1   What do you know about them? What are their interests and concerns?
2   Decide your strategic objectives – inform or persuade?

Overview

3   Decide the objective/ purpose/gain – what's in it for them?
4   Arrange the sequence of sub-topics or the questions you intend to address.

Summary

5   Prepare statements of the main messages for each sub-topic.
6   Decide on the one key message for the audience to take away – the signature.

Body

7   Identify the minimum

essential information for each topic.

8   Choose examples or other evidence to support that information.

9   Work out how these examples can be related to the audience.

10   Ensure that 7, 8 and 9 will support each main message.

11   Formulate some rhetorical questions and decide where to use them.

12   Introduce humour, gossip and asides as appropriate.

Finally

13   Prepare visuals to deliver the message and provide cues.

14   Have at least one practice run.

Remember

The 'winning' presentation is well-balanced:

- **Informing**   **25%**
- **Integrating**   **25%**
- **Elaborating**   **25%**
- **Emphasizing**   **25%**

Supplementary information
and examples

Why analyse your audience?

Your presentations must have an audience focus. Adopting a presenter-focused approach will turn you into a boring 'little professor' (see page 143). Some years ago, an audience of financial advisers and trustees attended the product launch of an Italian investment fund. The presenter spent 20 minutes on a general overview of the Italian economy. The audience, although perhaps marginally interested in the Italian economy, were not being convinced of the merits of the fund. They wanted to know the potential benefits to them and the answers to three specific questions:

1 Why invest in Italy?
2 Why use an Italian-based company?
3 Why choose the presenting company to manage the investments?

The presenter could have given a persuasive answer to each question:

1 To capitalize on the imminent privatizations of state-owned monopolies.
2 Because both the government and investors favour the use of Italian companies.
3 Because of their previous experience in share issues, their local knowledge and associations with banks, insurance companies and other financial institutions.

The presenter's mistake was to believe that an extensive demonstration of background knowledge would be a persuasive argument. This presentation might have been useful in an educative seminar to colleagues or other industry professionals but it failed to answer the key questions of the prospective clients.

How to analyse your audience

A proper audience focus needs analysis and understanding. This could entail research, talking to the audience themselves (they will appreciate your thoroughness) or by interviewing a third party who knows them. Educated guesses can also help. Use the following sample questions as a guide:

- What do you know about their age, gender, professional qualifications and experience?
- What are their specific interests – their situation, problems, issues and needs?
- If they are architects and designers, how will they be commissioned by their clients to choose your product and service – on price, functionality or environmentally sustainable materials?
- If they are a bank looking at software for trading systems, how many of them will have a complete understanding of the sophisticated technical features your software offers? Which of them has no technical expertise whatsoever but signs the cheques?
- If you are selling an emerging market to pension fund managers, have they ever suffered significant losses in one of these before?

Don't ask yourself, 'What do I want to tell them?'. Instead ask yourself, 'If I were in their position what would I want to hear?'.

There is much to get wrong, so find out what will help to get it right.

Two alternative strategies

Presentations have one of two specific objectives: either to inform the audience – a 'need to know' message – or to persuade them to commit to a particular course of action – a 'need to act' message. A common misconception is to believe that there are only minor differences in construction between the two. In fact, for either to be successful you will need to select the appropriate strategy for construction. Two distinct approaches were identified in our research, which looked at situations where presenters had the declared aim of gaining their audience's commitment to a course of action. Situations included external 'beauty parades', or pitches to existing and prospective clients, and managers presenting internally for their own departments seeking a budget allocation or to have their departmental strategy approved.

The first approach consisted of the presenters building up their case through a logically progressing argument to reach their conclusion – that is, whatever the action or demand was.

Although the presenters gave an introductory over-view, the specific action point was only implied in it and was vague, rather than specific. In the second approach the presenters clearly stated the specific action or demand as part of the initial overview and then followed it with a simple justification.

In a persuasive situation which strategy would you choose?

When asked, most presenters opt for the first strategy as the one most likely to lead to success. However, our research shows that in over 80 per cent of the cases where presenters chose to use this approach in a persuasive situation they failed to win the commitment they wanted. It is in fact the second strategy that has the better chance of succeeding, with a typical success rate of between 60 and 70 per cent.

Stating your action up-front

To understand why the second strategy is so successful, imagine that you are pitching to your finance committee for a small marketing budget. Using the first strategy of building up your case by logical argument you might start by giving the background to the exposure or opportunity and then begin to build up your case progessively. Research shows that if you adopt this approach, you will be confronted by interventions stimulated by your logical argument.

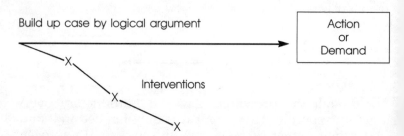

The case for your marketing budget might be queried on the grounds of your analysis of national versus regional differences, your sample size or your chosen socioeconomic categories, with the result that you will be deflected away from your logical argument into discussing minor points and lose precious time defending areas of detail. Indeed, you may never reach your conclusion – the chair of the finance committee will tell you how fascinating your idea sounds, but as time is short today why not go back and extend the sample size, work on those socioeconomic categories, and come back to re-present at a later date? Your pitch fails to win the decision and, in the intervening period, priorities may change as new issues take precedence. Moreover, going back to pitch a second time you will start at a disadvantage because the committee will have already formed preconceptions.

To illustrate the second strategy, where you state your demand or the specific action required up-front, imagine the same situation but place yourself in the position of a member of the finance committee. An executive from the marketing department starts his presentation by saying: 'I'm here today to win your approval of £30 000 expenditure on a small marketing campaign. . . . May I have the money please?'

What will be your reaction? Normally it would be either 'No' or 'Why? Justify your requirement'.

In the former instance, the presenter asks 'Why not?' and in the latter the presenter concisely answers the question 'Why', presenting the principal argument for approving the money and concludes with 'Now may I have the money please?'

This simple example may be unrealistic and exaggerated (can you imagine asking for budget with no justification?) but it illustrates the shift in dynamic from the presenter having to make the case for, to the committee having to decide the case against – *unaided*. The marketing executive provides no ammunition for his audience to attack the arguments and, consequently, the committee has much less basis for refusal.

Limiting the arguments is crucial. The strategy has two stages. First, take the time and make the effort to decide what the *minimum credible justification* is.

Too much information and you risk stimulating those

destructive interventions. Too little, and your case will not be credible.

Second, brainstorm the likely questions and develop the answers. What questions does your minimum justification not address?

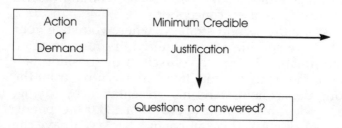

Running a rehearsal will also reveal the questions that your presentation is likely to stimulate.

Feedback from clients who have used this approach liken it to an examination where they open the paper and realize that they have researched and revised all the right questions. What first seemed a daunting prospect becomes quite exhilarating. One of the School's clients, a lawyer, was presenting to a local authority. Her entire presentation was about the importance to the authority of conducting a full insurance audit. She made no mention of her firm throughout, but the first question she was asked – the one to which each member of the authority's committee wanted an answer – was, 'Why should we use your firm?'. Fully expecting this question, and therefore prepared for it, she gave a brief, confident answer. In relegating the issue to the question-and-answer session, she was able to deal with it more powerfully and, consequently, her firm won the business. Most presenters would view this as a radical tactic, but there is often more prestige to be gained by providing a confident answer on a subject than trying to deal with it in the presentation. Predicting questions and rehearsing answers is a large part of the persuasive strategy (but more difficult in the logical build-up approach where questions become less predictable and the subsequent answers become less confidently delivered).

In terms of results, presenters who use this strategy move from a very low level of success, winning perhaps only one in five pitches, to much higher conversion rates – some in excess of four out of every five.

Validation of the strategy

Research into the effectiveness of negotiators revealed a common fallacy about negotiation – the 'weight of evidence' theory. This theory maintains that if you put forward many reasons for a particular course of action and your opponent can only think of a few, then through the weight of evidence you will win.

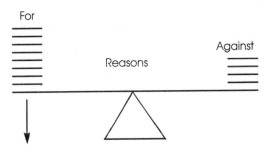

This theory is of course flawed. Firstly, there is no weighting. You might produce 10, 15 or 20 reasons why you need the money for that marketing campaign only to find that the finance committee has just one reason for refusal that completely defeats all yours – there is no money left. However, weighting of the arguments is not the most common reason why the approach fails. When formulating multiple reasons for a particular course of action, you start out with the strongest, but the more reasons you devise the weaker your arguments become. In a negotiation (and in a persuasive pitch) it is the weakest arguments that are attacked, leading to the collapse of the entire case as the stronger reasons are discredited by association. The argument is therefore lost on its weakest point. This phenomenon is known as 'argument dilution'.

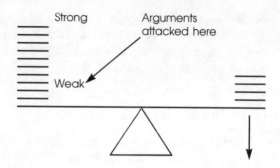

Research has shown that successful negotiators use fewer reasons per argument, sticking rigorously to the strongest reason and occasionally reaching for something equally strong to support it. In contrast, unsuccessful negotiators, who fail to reach a win–win conclusion, use a much greater number of reasons per argument – more than twice as many – and fall into the dilution trap.

The strength of the persuasive presentation strategy is that you present only the strong main argument whereas the build-up, informative strategy clouds the issue with weaker points and detail.

A good example of a weak point undermining a strong argument was the UK government's reason for blocking Britain's entry into the European Monetary System. Their one strong reason was 'loss of sovereignty'. Whatever the benefits or attractions of the EMS there was no real answer to the argument of sovereignty. However, a second reason was sometimes added, concerning inflation rates, which were not yet under control, the argument being 'the time is not right'. However, this argument did not strengthen the case; rather it diluted the strong argument of sovereignty. Suddenly, sovereignty was not immovable – it had a shelf life, a sell-by date by association with the secondary argument. One day the time *would* be right.

Using the persuasive approach

Keep your justification to a minimum, using a maximum of three arguments. Adhere to your strong arguments to avoid dilution. Do not try to answer all the possible questions within the presentation itself. All that does is obscure the strong reasons and, through dilution, cause your case to fail. The audience only needs to understand enough to say 'Yes'. (This is not cheating; you are not obscuring the real reasons with unnecessary detail, and any further understanding can be achieved in the discussion following the presentation of the case.)

The sequence of points is important. Use the 1-3-2 rule in sequencing. The most important or strongest argument should be presented first, when audience attention is at its highest. Audiences remember best the first and last things they hear – the phenomenon of primacy and recency – so put your weakest argument in the middle and your second strongest last. Moreover, ask yourself if you really need your weakest point – will it simply dilute your argument?

Using the informative/educational approach

If your messages are non-actionable, 'need-to-know', and your objective is to educate and inform, you want your audience to have a full understanding. The progressive build-up approach is the most appropriate in this situation.

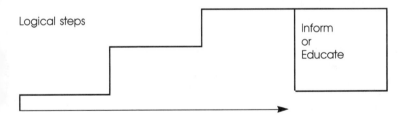

Interventions stimulated by the building approach form part of an audience's route to achieving full understanding. The presenter only needs to decide the size of each step, relative to the audience's ability. A specialist, or bright and articulate, audience can take relatively few and more complex steps. A less technically literate audience may need a more systematic and detailed route to achieve full understanding.

Presentations introducing a new IT system should be constructed differently for specialist audiences than for ordinary, non-technical end-users.

Need to know or need to act?

Be clear on your objective and beware of traditional thinking in the construction of your presentation.

Ask yourself how many of your presentations, in persuasive situations, have been simply informative in their structure?

The presentation content – a methodical approach

Why a method approach?

If you consider the typical feedback you might receive on your presentation it will tend to be highly subjective: 'I liked this' or 'I disliked that' or 'If I were you . . .'. The comments may be well-meaning but they are often conflicting and not easily actionable as they do not guide you in how to distinguish the truly effective parts of your presentation from the rest.

From our work with specialists in behaviour analysis and research into audience reactions, trends and preferences, we have evolved a method for producing effective content and messages. This method has been adopted successfully by thousands of presenters at all levels and disciplines, in a whole variety of situations from formal large audiences to small groups and one-to-one pitches.

The model comprises four main categories of activity: **informing, elaborating, integrating** and **emphasizing**. Everything you say in a presentation can be categorized into one of these four activities. Understanding what they mean and how they work together will give you the recipe for packaging an effective message.

Your presentation should be structured as follows:

- an overview
- the body containing main sub-topics
- a final summary of the key messages.

The overview – off to a flying start

The first few moments of a presentation are critical. What you say and how you behave will condition your audience's opinions and reactions to both you and your message. An audience makes up its mind very quickly so you have to get it right. It may be an old cliché, but you do not have a second chance to make a first impression. Therefore the design and delivery of the overview are pivotal to the success of your presentation.

There are many possible definitions of 'overview' – summary, précis, main recommendation, big picture, main points and so on. Thinking of the overview as the big picture, a useful analogy is that of a 'blueprint'. If the blueprint is wrong, then what you construct from it will be similarly flawed. Correct design of the overview is key. Get it wrong and the rest of your presentation will be wrong as a result. For an overview to be an effective blueprint for your presentation it should contain three identifiable components. The sequence of presenting these components may vary but the overview must include each of the following:

- a purpose
- a hook
- a map

The purpose

You should give a clear statement of purpose – what the presentation is intended to do for your audience. One of the common traps that presenters fall into is to use unspecific expressions such as 'We're here today to talk about . . .', 'This presentation will look at . . .' or 'My talk examines . . .'. These phrases are vague and do not tell the audience what the presentation is designed to do. A clear statement of purpose specifies your objective and explains that the presentation will 'give you an insight', or 'give you an understanding' or 'an appreciation'. These examples would apply where your intention is to educate or inform your audience. If your purpose is to persuade you might say 'We're here today to win your mandate', 'to secure your commitment' or 'to persuade you to approve this strategy'.

The hook

Another component is the hook, designed to seize attention by giving the audience the reasons why it should listen to you. An audience's attention may be distracted by other issues or preoccupations at any time. They may also have preconceived notions about you and your subject. These distractions, allied to the fact that listening is hard work, mean that if your audience is not presented with a good reason for paying attention, then it probably won't. The hook sells your audience on listening to what you're about to tell them. Conventional wisdom says that the more time you spend convincing your audience of the benefits of listening, the less time you will have to actually present. However, if you don't persuade them to listen in the first place they could miss everything else!

Design a hook of your own using one of the following techniques.

Opportunity

This technique is often used in general sales presentations to show the potential benefits to the audience. One stock sector was described as 'the most exciting and under-valued investment opportunity seen for the last four years'. On a less emphatic note, wealthy individuals attending a private banking seminar were offered the opportunity to 'save time and money'. A humorous variation of this hook by a sales director to pharmaceutical reps was the opening, 'If you can't sell more after listening to this – see a doctor'.

Enhanced opportunity

This is a similar technique to the above but uses an analogy, to which the audience can relate, to paint a familiar or simpler picture of a complex opportunity. Making the parallel between an audience's investment in their own domestic property and the commercial property investments of their business is one example. Financial advisers attending a conference at Gleneagles were offered investment management that would keep their clients' money 'on the fairway and not in the rough'.

Fear or threat

The 'pay attention, we'll be asking questions later' approach can play on the audience members' fear of personal exposure in front of the rest of the audience, clients or colleagues. Few audiences will wish to remain ignorant of an emerging market sector or a unique product or service if their own clients may be interested in it. This hook gives them a powerful incentive to pay attention. The possibility that their clients or colleagues will doubt their ability if they can't answer their questions on new developments is something to be avoided, it is therefore better to listen.

Decision criteria

This technique is used frequently in business pitches to show an understanding of the decision that has to be made: 'This presentation will answer the three questions that are uppermost in your mind. Why should you consolidate your IT services? Why choose us to do it? And, why is now the time to do it?

This hook creates empathy with your audience because it implies that you are looking at the situation from their perspective and avoids a 'product blast' or the 'talking brochure' syndrome. It can also be used in educative situations or seminars by considering the principal questions on your subject to which the audience will want answers.

Framing the questions on your audience's mind shows that you are on the same wavelength and are seeing the situation from their perspective and not just from your own.

Mystery

Favoured by TV stations to induce viewers to tune in, this technique is designed to whet your audience's appetite for something yet to be revealed: 'Your specification document outlined some key objectives. I'm here to show you that we can not only meet your stated objectives but also your hidden objectives too.' (Audience reaction: 'I wonder what those hidden objectives are?')

Another example is: 'There's a new dealer starting work this week. This dealer will never go off sick, won't make a bad deal, doesn't get paid and won't join you in the pub after work.' (Audience reaction: 'Who is this?')

Showstopper

An unexpected startling statement or powerful rhetorical question at the outset will arrest the audience's attention.

'Fellow directors and shareholders, I have to tell you that our company is bankrupt. . . . However, the good news is we are not as bankrupt as our competitors.'

'This company is on target, on target for nil revenue, no customers and zero business . . . unless we change our strategy, that is.'

'Ask yourselves this question – could you afford to live on the equivalent of a student grant? . . . Probably not, but that is what living on the state pension alone actually means . . . .'

The map

The third component of your overview is the map. This is the agenda headings of the one, two, or a maximum of three key sub-topics that you intend to cover or key questions that you intend to answer. The term 'map' has connotations of a route, a direction, and of identifiable journey stops along the way which, in this case, are represented by the sub-topics.

If you attempt to cover more than three sub-topics, each

with its own point or message, it is unlikely that your audience will absorb all your points.

In our own analytical work, we have shown a short three-and-a-half minute videotaped presentation to a sample of 2500 people. It is well structured and its four key messages are clearly delivered. When asked to recall the speaker's messages most remembered only one or two points, a small number recalled three, but just two out of the 2500 sample could recall all four points.

Sequencing the topics

From the analysis of that video it is also important to note the frequency of the messages that were recalled. All of the sample recalled the first point and a majority the first and last. Fewer remembered the middle points and less than 50 recalled the second point. The lessons here are simple: **never present more than three topics** and present them in the sequence of **most important first, second most important last** and the **least important second**, sandwiched in the middle – **the 1-3-2 rule**.

Remember:

The overview is your blueprint – challenge its concepts and your own thinking before fleshing out the detailed content of the sub-topics. But, by including the **purpose**, a **hook** and the **map** in the overview, you can prepare and motivate your audience to follow your presentation. They will be primed by your statement of purpose, motivated to listen by the hook, and aware of the topics and sequence that your presentation will follow.

The body – fleshing out your sub-topics

It is in developing the content of the sub-topics that the method formula is applied, using the main activity categories of informing, elaborating, integrating and emphasizing. Understanding these terms and their inter-relation gives you the formula for success.

Informing – the basic content

Whilst the overview is a structural component and delivered at the outset of your presentation, the other two informing activities in our method can occur throughout. They are defined as follows.

Annotating or labelling

If you give titles or numbers to the information you present, you break the mass of the content down into identifiable, memorable pieces. 'Three identifiable components of successful implementation' and 'two problems to be aware of and avoid' are examples of annotating, using numbers to make remembering easier. You can also use labels such as 'Let me ask you a question . . .', 'To give you an example . . .' and 'So in conclusion . . .' to tell your audience what is coming next and break the information into identifiable parts.

Making statements of fact or opinion

Such statements comprise the basic views, ideas or opinions that you need in order to convey your message. Be careful not to include too many of these factual or opinion statements in your presentation. Audiences cannot cope with large amounts of facts and opinions which are difficult to absorb aurally, and make a presentation boring. They have difficulty imagining facts, visualizing and getting a feel for them and it then becomes increasingly difficult to concentrate and keep taking facts in. Be selective and reduce this factual information to the minimum essential. Use the other activity categories, especially elaborating, to bring this minimum to life.

Detailed factual content is better presented in written handout form so that people can study it at their own pace, revise and check; the oral presentation should be concerned with messages not detailed facts.

Elaborating – the proof and evidence

When someone says to you that they 'hear what you're saying', the codicil is usually 'but . . .'. You can infer, in fact, that they don't agree with you. By contrast, when someone says to you that they 'see what you mean' this indicates that you have made your point. The greatest proportion of the population is visually orientated, so the art of an oral presentation is to create images for your audience. The purpose of elaboration is to get your audience to see what you mean, to help them visualize what you are saying and to offer proof of your statements of fact.

You can bring facts to life by using any of the following four devices.

Examples and analogies

Use examples and analogies that are tangible and at a level suitable for the audience. To show how large a continent Latin America is, a presenter recounted how it had taken her five hours to fly from the east coast to the west, the equivalent of flying from London to the Middle East. Prospective clients of a private banking service, having been informed of the quarterly charges, were told that the same sum would buy them for example, the *Financial Times* every day for the same period and that, either way, this amount would buy them access to a whole range of financial information. Would they prefer to try and make sense of it themselves or would they rather the bank did this for them? There is only one thing worse than facts – figures. Putting them in context this way helps your audience to visualize the amounts.

A presenter talking about the explosive growth in computer software could have gathered all sorts of statistics but made his point simply by saying: 'If five years ago you had taken every available piece of software and laid it on the ground in front of you, you could only have covered the penalty area on the football pitch at Wembley stadium. If you undertook the same exercise today, the software would cover the whole pitch and the terraces.' This analogy enabled his audience to visualize the growth in computer software.

Be careful, however, with analogies. They must make sense and be credible to your audience. One fund manager once lost an important deal by using a cricketing analogy, which had worked well on previous occasions, to an audience of American clients, who had no idea what he was talking about.

Another form of verbal visualization is the puzzle-solution format. Once, referring to the Labour Party's manifesto, the Conservative prime minister called it the 'iceberg manifesto'. What did she mean by this puzzle? Answer: nine-tenths of its socialism was hidden below the surface.

Visual illustrations

Giving the audience something it can physically see helps to reinforce the message. Photographs, drawings, graphs, histograms, pie-charts all aid elaboration. For details of visual techniques and layouts, see page 156.

Third-party references

Third-party references, such as credible names or case histories that your audience would be familiar with, especially from within their own industry sector, profession or business, are a good source of proof. Another source would be recognized authorities – for example, any periodical from, say, *Which* magazine to *Planned Savings* – to provide independent proof to reinforce the case for a particular consumer durable or financial product.

Experience and expertise

Your own experience and expertise in the subject area will carry weight when presenting. Anecdotal evidence is a source of proof but be careful not to overuse this device or you risk being perceived as a 'when I' bore.

If your audience can visualize what you are saying, they are more likely to understand it, believe, and consequently accept it. However the basis of elaboration must be proof of your statements of fact and opinion.

Integrating – the 'you factor'

To maintain interest and relevance your audience must feel involved, otherwise it will question the relevance of your presentation. Integrating, often referred to as the 'you factor' can best be described as 'relating' – relating parts of the content of your presentation to each other or, more importantly, relating your material to the audience. Of the four behaviours in the category of integration, two are for relating to the audience and two are for interrelating parts of the material.

Relating to the audience's experiences

Relate your examples or other elaboration to the audience's experiences so that they have a strong resonance and connection. This can be most successfully achieved if you can identify experiences they have in common. If they are all independent financial advisers, for example, they will have been subject to increasing regulatory and compliance procedures over the last seven years. In a manufacturing context, your audience is likely to have had all their procedures rewritten to conform to quality standard BS5750, a customer requirement.

 If you cannot identify work experiences your audience have in common, use everyday life occurrences or current affairs.

Relating to the audience's situation

Telling the audience specifically how the content of your presentation will affect them in their job, career, department or company is your main objective in any sales or persuasive pitch. So the independent financial advisers mentioned above would relate strongly to anything that reduced paperwork and let them spend more time face-to-face with their clients, such as a computerized product selection and administration service. Similarly, manufacturers would be prepared to streamline their procedures to accommodate a Just-in-Time approach if they perceived that, like BS5750, it was something on which all their customers would soon insist.

Try to relate both to experience and situation. If all your examples relate to your audience's situation it will sound like the oversell. If it all relates to experience then they may well feel dissatisfied but still unsure, asking 'How is this going to help me?'

Without integration your presentation can fall well short of its target. An extreme example of this concerns two consecutive annual sales conferences. The first year's after-dinner speaker was a well known game show comedian who went to the trouble of finding out the names of the directors and principal staff and some of the associated stories that had passed into company folklore. He integrated these into his act and brought the (full) house down. In stark contrast, the following year an equally famous comedian merely reproduced for his audience his latest TV act. He lasted three minutes before the first of many breadrolls was thrown – so it was goodnight from him! Your audience (hopefully) won't physically throw things at you, but if you fail to integrate they may well switch off and throw things mentally.

Using links

Other integrating behaviour relates more to the material. Use links to show how different parts of your presentation relate to each other. Examples are: 'If the problems we've just seen are getting worse, then the need for a prompt effective solution grows stronger every day. The solution I propose is as follows . . .'or 'If you found our previous efforts helpful, then wait until you see what we're planning next!'

Referring to earlier issues

This is another way to integrate your material: for example, 'As I said earlier . . .' You might also refer to any previous meetings, discussions or significant events that have a bearing on your presentation such as 'If you recall at our previous meeting you outlined your circumstances . . .'.

Remember, the audience is there to hear how what you have to say relates to them. Make sure you tell them – employ the 'you factor'.

Emphasizing – making your points heard and remembered

Because your audience can only cope with a limited number of messages, you need to use emphasizing behaviour to ensure that they retain your key messages, not others picked up at random and certainly not contradictory ones. You need to make your points audibly strike home. There are four activities that you can use for emphasis.

Making statements of importance

The first such device is to cue your audience to listen by making statements of importance to tell the audience that the important things *are* important. Use superlatives to make the point: 'I can't emphasize this strongly enough . . .', 'This is most significant' or 'The key/critical/vital/ crucial thing to remember is . . .'. Do not assume that the significant points are obvious to your audience. Important benefits – higher profits, economies of scale or more effective use of time – can be buried amongst descriptions of the features of your product or service. You may feel reluctant to use such phrasing for fear of sounding ridiculous or evangelical. This is an inaccurate perception; you would have to use this type of language to great excess to sound ridiculous or 'over the top'. In fact, your audience will interpret this behaviour as strength of feeling and conviction.

Finally, remember that listening is hard work and your audience may lapse into a passive mode at any time. Using this behaviour, – this emphatic language – will seize their attention and make them tune back in for that (all-important) point. Experienced orators often use this type of language two or three times before delivering their particular point.

Summarizing

Summarize at the beginning of your presentation (the map) and after every sub-topic or key point. Summarize at the end, gathering together the one, two or three key messages and the overall main message – the 'signature'.

Summarize also in case of emergency, when you lose your way or become sidetracked. As summarizing is a natural behaviour, your audience are unlikely to notice and it will remind you of where you were and put you back on course.

To make your summaries more forceful try using a 'soundbite' – a short memorable phrase or slogan which encapsulates the point you're making. Soundbites are popular with politicians, the media and advertisers to convey a strong message in the shortest possible time. The following seven soundbites – 'Peace in our time', 'Blood, toil, tears and sweat', 'You've never had it so good', 'The white heat of technology', 'The winter of discontent', 'There is no alternative' and 'Back to basics' – chart a short political history of Britain since 1939. Watch any commercial break on TV – most will contain at least one soundbite.

Some of the most effective soundbites and summaries

use the notorious rule of three: three occurrences of a particular thing, quality or even a letter: 'What this all adds up to is experience. It's length of experience, for more than fifty years. It's breadth of experience, across the world and . . .' (can you guess what's coming next?) '. . . it's depth of experience, at all levels of the organization'. This makes a more powerful summary than simply using the term 'experience' once. Another more succinct example is 'Worldwide, world class and working for you' – a memorable soundbite. An analyst talking about the evolution of the Chinese economy and government intervention said 'Remember its development as a cycle of *Boom, Bust, Readjust*'. The leader of the opposition replied to the earlier example of the prime minister's 'iceberg manifesto' puzzle by seeming to agree – another puzzle – and then giving an answer in threes: 'Its really cool, very tough, and totally unsinkable.'

Soundbites are often much more difficult to formulate than they are to forget. Try adapting an existing one to your needs or look one up in a dictionary of quotations.

Using rhetorical questions

The rhetorical question is another technique that can be used to give emphasis. Questions demand answers and thus the participation of the audience. But direct questions can be quite threatening, particularly in larger audiences. Using rhetorical questions achieves audience participation without the fear of exposure and without exposing you to interruptions. Preface your rhetorical question with phrases that will help to prevent unwanted responses. For example, say 'Ask yourselves this question, how can you, as investment advisers, allow this opportunity to go by?' and then pause while your audience consider the question. This behaviour will both grip their attention and induce them to work with the material, thereby ensuring that they remember it. The pause is crucial, otherwise a finely crafted piece of emphasis may be wasted.

Using humour

Using humour gives potent emphasis because it is so memorable. However, unless you link your humour to your message there is a danger that your humour will be remembered at its expense. Perhaps this is best illustrated by the ex-chairman of a national jewellery retail chain. Having now lost his position, several million pounds of the company value and the company brand name he has cause to regret his humorous off-the-cuff, but widely reported, remark about the quality of one of the items they sold.

An example of a much more effective use of humour was the chief executive who was explaining his company philosophy. To fix the key message in the audience's mind he related how, on leaving his house earlier that day, his wife had asked him what would be the subject of his address to the conference. 'Small is beautiful,' he replied. 'Never mind dear,' she sympathized 'I still love you.'

Remember, emphasis will draw attention to your key points and should make them audibly different and memorable!

The summary – the final message

The important thing to remember here is to summarize what you have actually said, not what you talked about. A list of the topics you covered in your presentation will not convey your message.

Compare these:

'So I've told you about the size, the aesthetics and the capabilities of our product.'

'So our product is big, it's beautiful and it works under water.'

The former reminds the audience of the topics of your

presentation. The latter combines the message from each topic into one main message – the 'signature'.

This signature should refer back to the gain or hook as stated in the overview – the opportunity defined, the decision made, the mystery solved. For example, if you had used a fear hook, the fear of being unable to answer client questions, the signature may go '. . . and that should put you in a good position to handle those questions from your clients – thank you for listening.' If it were an opportunity hook of saving time and money the signature would be '. . . and that will save you a significant amount of time and money – thank you very much.'

In summary

In the body of your presentation use the following activities:

- **informing** – the basic content
- **elaborating** – proving the content through visualization
- **integrating** – the 'you factor' relating to your audience
- **emphasis** – highlighting the key points and messages.

Now that you understand the terminology and definitions of the categories, how do they become a method formula or recipe?

The importance of a balanced presentation

All the above behaviours that make up our verbal model are observable. Research, and the continuing success of our clients, prove that there is a definite pattern to the activities that make a presentation effective.

The pattern you need to achieve makes an even

contribution to each category of behaviour. In other words, 25 per cent of all your activity will be in each category: informing, integrating, elaborating and emphasizing. To understand why it is important to achieve this balance, imagine the effect on your audience of an out-of-balance presentation when the categories go to extremes.

Presentations that are *high in informing* activity will normally contain a large proportion of facts, ideas, views and opinions. Audiences tend to lose interest during these, finding that the presentation is boring and blaming you, the presenter. What they mean is that the content is hard to digest.

At the other extreme, the audience will view a presentation that has a *low factual content* as superficial, and may question your knowledge of the subject. This may not mean that it was not enjoyable – it could be entertaining and humorous – but as one individual said, 'Great show but where's the beef?'.

High integration is typical of sales presentations and is usually characterized by excessive references to the audience's situation: 'Here's what's in it for you.' Audiences react in the same way you and I do when we feel that we're being oversold – they back off and become suspicious. A *lack of integration* leaves the audience wondering what the presentation has to do with them. It is seen as irrelevant. The chairman of a merchant bank addressing a conference overlooked this. The audience, directors of small to medium-sized manufacturing companies, soon lost interest in a presentation about billion pound financing schemes for the Channel Tunnel. They were unable to see how it related to them.

A whole host of problems is associated with excessive elaboration – numerous anecdotes, examples, analogies and third-party references. *Overelaboration* can make the information content of a presentation seem superficial, or it can suppress the message. This is typified by 'the little professor' syndrome. One such presenter was speaking on the subject of wine to an expectant, attentive and interested audience but, after the fourth 'fascinating example' of the peculiar effect on the grape harvest that he had witnessed on his holiday in Bordeaux in the mid-1950s, all he had was an audience who wanted to move on to the wine-tasting.

However, if there is *insufficient elaboration* then your presentation will lack credibility. It will be incredible in the true sense of the word. (So if your audience gives you such feedback as 'Incredible presentation and I really hear what you say', you will know exactly what they mean.)

Too much emphasis has the opposite effect. If all the points in your presentation are so important, your audience will find it difficult to identify the salient ones. Equally, the more you repeat the significance of one particular factor, the more hostile your audience will become – you are treating them like children! *Fail to give due emphasis* and your audience will pick out a message at random, and it's unlikely to be the one you wanted them to remember!

The chances of giving a balanced presentation, with about 25 per cent of the total activity in each of the four categories of behaviour are low unless you understand what each one means, how they work together and, most importantly, the serious problems resulting from including too much or too little of any of them.

Presenters who are untutored in our method approach tend to exhibit a pattern of high informing activity, low integrating , high elaborating activity and low emphasizing. The high categories are the presenter-related ones – it's the presenter's overview, their labels, their information, their examples and analogies and their experience that they're using. The presentation is centred on the presenter. To achieve the right balance, therefore, you have to alter the focus and ask yourself:

- What is important to the audience?
- How can I make sure that they go away with the right messages?
- How can I make my presentation relate to them?

In this way, you move away from a presenter-led towards

an audience-focused presentation. You consider not what you want to tell them, but what they need to hear.

Two examples illustrate this typical problem. An actuary presenting to an audience of pension fund trustees about the benefits of a new index fund spent 20 minutes on the differences between stratified sampling, optimization and full replication. This demonstrated his expertise but did nothing to answer the audience's questions: 'Why should we adopt indexation? 'Why choose this particular method?', 'Why choose these people to manage it?' The second example is that of an economist addressing a seminar to advisers about investment opportunities in Spain in the next two years. His half-hour address on the pre-Franco economy did not really connect with what they wanted to hear.

The key is to change the focus from what you want to say to what the audience want to hear.

How to ensure a balanced presentation

As stated previously, an effective presentation is one where equal attention is paid to the basic content, the associated proof, relating this to the audience and stressing the key messages. To ensure that this balance is maintained you need to consider the composition. The following examples are balanced equally across the four categories of behaviour:

1   City offices are expensive [*statement*]. The floor space occupied by your desk costs £12 000 a year to rent [*audience related example* – not just any old desk, it's *yours*]. So the important point is that you need to generate £12 000 each year simply to pay for the space your desk occupies [*emphasis*].
2   Our company and yours work in identical fashion [*statement*]. You analyse your markets very carefully before developing a new product to ensure a good return on your investment. Similarly we use our depth of research capability to ensure that the stocks

selected for portfolios like yours, stocks like these (list) will give a good return [*audience related examples*]. We understand your business – the principles on which we work are the same. Therefore we can work together successfully [*emphasis*].

Because of your expertise, informing and elaborating will come naturally to you. It is integration and emphasis, the relationship between your expertise and the audience's needs, that you will need to think hard about.

If your presentation is made up of sub-topics which themselves are balanced across the four activity categories, then the whole presentation will be similarly balanced and therefore much more effective at conveying your message to your audience.

Many of the delegates on our courses remember it like a mantra: fact-example-integrate-summarize repeated again and again. That is, for each statement that you make you ask yourself the following questions. Where is the visualization or proof of it? How/where does it relate to my audience and why am I saying it? What is the point?

If you can't answer the last question should you be making that particular statement in the first place?

The non-verbal aspects of presenting

There are many aspects of delivery style and many tips and techniques to improve your public speaking prowess. Several famous presenters are well known for their idiosyncratic delivery styles; these qualities are attractive to some, and annoying to other members of their audiences in about equal measure. So what can they do? If they cease their arm-waving, excessive modulation and odd turns of phrase just to satisfy those who are distracted and don't appreciate them, then the people who enjoy that style of delivery will be disappointed. The point is that audience reception will be no better, nor worse. The key to your non-verbal delivery style is to be yourself. In all business presentations your audience are looking for those intangible qualities of personal chemistry and confidence. If you put on an act it is, in effect, a deception and will cause you problems sooner or later. The non-verbal method will take account of any personal idiosyncracies and give you common things to look out for, helping you to project your own personality and style.

The aspects of your non-verbal delivery behaviour to be aware of fall into four areas:

- positioning
- sight lines and scanning
- voice and delivery
- mannerisms and dress.

Positioning yourself to move and address your audience

Standing behind a lectern or sitting at a desk will be unhelpful in two ways – it will restrict the audience's view of you and it will restrict your ability to move. This is ironic when you consider that the organizers of your meeting or presentation have supplied the desk or lectern to *help* you. A lectern is often provided in a large auditorium where bigger images and gestures are usually needed. But, with a lectern, your audience, many of whom will be sitting quite far away, will have only your head and shoulders to focus on. Your small static image hidden behind a barrier doesn't lend itself to reaching out and making contact with them. Come out from behind that barrier to the front or side and you present a larger image, and if you want to move around you can. Try to swap a static microphone for a clip-on, but remember to remove it before you leave the stage. Many speakers have been embarrassed by their own activities and comments they have made off-stage, forgetting the microphone was still clipped on and live.

Your degree of movement depends on the size of the group – do not stand over members of a small audience of, say, six people and expect them to take in what you are saying. They will be uncomfortable and disturbed by your close proximity. Rather, shift your body weight as you stand to make obvious physical gestures indicating those to the left or right or in the centre. For larger presentations you can move around the stage, in the manner of many entertainers, 'working' the different parts of your audience. Your aim is to involve each member of the audience to give them the feeling of being spoken to directly, to achieve that closeness, that contact and that chemistry.

Desks are a similar obstacle. Many presenters will say that they feel more comfortable seated. They may well do, but this position diminishes the focal point for the audience and introduces difficulties of control for the presenter – it is all too easy for the presentation to degenerate into a sit-down 'chat'. Not only does sitting inhibit correct breathing, it also makes it more difficult to exert control and influence over the group. Sitting is a 'joining' behaviour and will invite more interruptions and discussions, which may well obscure your messages and lead you off at a tangent. Stand to separate yourself from the group, to focus and control them. Sit to join them at their level. There is a good case for standing during the presentation and then sitting for the subsequent discussion, but be prepared to stand up again to regain control.

There is a need to exercise some judgement about social norms and the appropriateness of standing but, as a general rule, stand and deliver with space to move and project to your audience.

Sight lines and scanning – to see and be seen

Being able to see and to be seen is another aspect that determines your positioning. How many times have you found yourself presenting in a room totally unsuited to the size of the audience or in a packed boardroom with members gathered around a long narrow boardroom table? You may dearly wish to relocate, remove the furniture or at least rearrange it, but these may not be practical solutions. Whatever happens, do not move forward to project to the back of the 'U' shape formed by the audience. If you come forward in this way you could exclude those people arranged to the side or even behind you. They may well feel ignored and lose interest, possibly conferring amongst themselves. Position yourself (with your back to the wall if necessary) so that you can see everyone in a natural scan.

The key word in relation to scanning is *everyone*. It's very easy to become transfixed on one individual, such as the friendly face. However, just because someone is smiling and nodding doesn't mean they're on your side. That frozen grin may be to hide their embarrassment at all the attention you're giving them. Equally, a chief executive won't necessarily have the final say – their colleagues' expert opinions may be more valued than their own. If you direct your delivery exclusively to the CEO in these circumstances what will the others conclude having been ignored for most of the presentation?

Every member of your audience has attended for a reason, so include them all in your delivery. Make eye contact with each of them at random intervals. Because staring is a primitive aggressive gesture, eye contact causes some presenters to feel uncomfortable. Avoid this discomfort by focusing on the area of forehead immediately above the bridge of the nose rather than looking in the eye. This gives the impression of eye contact without that awkward discomforting feeling, or risk of 'locking on' to one single individual.

Wherever possible do not present with your back to a window or strong light source. This makes eye contact more difficult, silhouetted as you are, and can be rather intimidating as well as tiring for the audience. Also you may well have a topic of real interest to your audience, but no matter how scintillating your presentation, there will always be the potential for something more interesting happening outside behind you. Window cleaners can be particularly entertaining! Avoid this unwelcome competition. Women presenters especially beware of standing in front of a strong light source since it can make lightweight clothing transparent.

The issue of sight lines also applies to your visuals. Ensure that your audience has a clear view of both you and your visual aids or images. A common error made by presenters using an overhead projector is to stand next to it and read from the bed of the machine. This will invariably obstruct a section of the audience's view of the visuals. Whatever type of equipment or aid you are using, stand to the side so that your audience can see the images. Always try to maintain a triangular formation of you, your audience and the visual screen.

The important thing to remember is that failure to make visual contact with your audience will send the wrong signals: the sceptical might view it as an indication that you are not wholly truthful. 'Look me in the eyes when you tell me that.' Attention to sight lines and scanning helps you do just that and generates a greater feeling of confidence and chemistry.

Voice

What is it that enables the opera singer to sing with such volume and clarity for a whole performance night after night? How does the regimental sergeant major bark his orders at such a volume that the squadron's ears hurt? The answer lies in *breathing*. Correct breathing is needed to generate volume and resonance from the diaphragm and chest. If you study any martial arts, tai-chi or yoga, this is what you will be taught. Breathing in through the nose as you push your stomach out will expand your rib-cage and lower your diaphragm, the muscular partition between the chest and the abdomen. This will fill both lungs. As you exhale whilst speaking you can control your voice by tightening your stomach muscles to give extra clarity and audibility.

There are a number of associated advantages to breathing properly. You will not strain your throat and voice by shouting, and your mouth won't dry up. Dry throat, a common problem, is usually caused by incorrect or shallow breathing. More importantly, this technique keeps your blood rich in oxygen so that you feel more relaxed when presenting. Nerves, anxiety and panic attacks are often a physiological reaction to shallow breathing. Finally, correct breathing can help in terms of pace – you won't need to rush to finish a phrase because you're running out of breath. If you are breathing correctly you should feel your chest and head resonating to the sound of your voice.

Pace

You should pace your delivery much slower than normal conversation speed, because your audience can't take in your content as fast as you can deliver it. If you feel as though you are speaking at normal conversation speed then you probably are talking too fast. Try lengthening the vowels, which give your words greater clarity, and also slow the pace. One simple tip is to imagine that you are talking to an audience of foreigners. This will help you to speak more slowly and enunciate the words better. Apart from slowing down so that your audience can follow you, there are a couple of other advantages. First, a slower pace gives you more thinking time, to consider what you will say next, and how to phrase it. Second, it adds more weight and lends authority to what you are saying. Your messages seem more considered and come across as the result of careful deliberation. Slowing down gives you and your messages *gravitas*.

Modulation

Many nationalities have natural modulation in their speech – the Scots, the Irish and the Italians, to name but a few, have a sing-song quality which makes their voices attractive to listen to. The note in the voice rises and falls in contrast to the more monotone sound of certain other regional accents. Hearing your voice as it actually sounds to others can be a shock (you normally only hear it amplified by the bones in your head). If you listen to your voice and realise that it sounds too monotonous use a simple media technique for developing modulation. If you listen to the delivery of current affairs anchor-people, news readers and other presenters you will hear them put the stress, place the inflection or change their tone on every third or fifth syllable or word irrespective of what that word or syllable is. The technique is not for emphasis but to give rhythm. To familiarize yourself with the technique practise reading poetry or write your presentation out in full, marking the words or syllables to be modulated or inflected.

Pauses

Paradoxically, your voice can be most effective when you are not using it. One of the most powerful devices in presentation is the pause – the pause for effect, for emphasis and to let the audience assimilate what you've just said. The perceived dangers with the pause are that someone may ask a question, interrupt you or think you've lost your way. All of these could happen if the pause were too long but, in actual fact, the pause is almost invariably too short. This is because your impression of the length of the pause is different from that of your audience. What seems like an eternity to you hardly registers as a break or punctuation mark with your audience. The only way to achieve a pause of the right length is to count to five, to yourself.

Remember, just because you use your voice without thinking in conversation, don't assume you can use it in a similar manner in your presentation. You must consciously use your speaking voice in a presentation.

Mannerisms and dress

Be yourself

Avoid any kind of theatricality. In other words, do not put on an act which is alien to your personality. Any attempt to appear overconfident will have a hollow ring to it. Be yourself and project your own personality. It is *you* they are buying; an act is a deception that you may live to regret. If you are a natural gesticulator, that's fine, but don't imitate other presenters' techniques – you may not be able to carry them off in the same way to the same effect.

Appearance

There is a school of thought that says the more interesting you look the more attention your audience will pay you. Flamboyant dressers especially believe this. Earrings like candelabras, garishly patterned ties, buttonholes and outrageous jewellery on your lapel are some examples of the exotic accessories that distract the audience's attention. Anything that takes their eyes off your face will detract from your delivery. In terms of conveying confidence creating that chemistry and getting your personality across, your face is *you*.

Many well known presenters make statements by the way they dress. They are already famous and have more than enough ego and personality for their words to compete with their appearance. Is your personality big enough for your message to compete successfully with your appearance?

Hands

Of all the questions we are asked by presenters 'What will I do with my hands?' is the most common. Keep them empty and free of pens, pointers and other things to fiddle with or use to threaten the audience. These are distracting. Direct attention to the screen with your hands and use them for illustration, dramatic effect and emphasis in as energetic a fashion as you normally do. When you're not using them in such a purposeful way, keep them loosely together in front of you, slightly above waist height. This is the 'home' position for your hands – it keeps the hands still, looks natural and doesn't send inappropriate signals to your audience. Avoid the following:

- *Hands behind the back*. You will either look like a wine waiter, ready to take the order or a naughty schoolboy, suspiciously hiding something behind you.
- *Hands by your sides*. You will seem lifeless and lacking in energy or resemble a sentry on duty.
- *The 'free-kick' position*. Clasping the hands together in front of the body protecting the groin, is a common position for both men and women presenters. A favourite stance at the start of the presentation or when you offer to take questions, it shows that you feel vulnerable and defensive.
- *Hands in the pockets*. This is sometimes known as the 'best-man's speech' position. If there are coins and keys in the pockets the temptation is to jingle them. If there are no coins or keys it can look even worse.

Practise the 'home' position. It feels unnatural at first but looks fine and has no unwelcome connotations. Note how many television presenters use this position for their hands.

Habits

We are all prone to 'um', 'er', 'ah' and scratch ourselves, but there is a natural, normal socially acceptable level that usually goes unnoticed. Similarly, you may have favourite words and phrases like 'basically', 'at the end of the day' and 'OK'. If you use any of these to excess, your audience will become aware of them as repetitive habits, start listening for them and counting them off. Such habits are often used to fill silences. It is better to mentally count through the silence than distract your audience with these kind of mannerisms.

Look, sound and act the part of yourself as presenter.

The objective of the non-verbal method

Quite simply it is *contact* with your audience that you are trying to establish and maintain. Ideally,100 per cent contact with 100 per cent of your audience 100 per cent of the time would be the aim. But this is impossible – you can only possibly achieve that level of contact on a one-to-one basis. Nevertheless your objective is to get as close to it as you possibly can.

You can do this by removing or minimizing anything that will create a barrier such as desks and lecterns. Distractions – both your own fidgeting, tapping or exotic accessories, and furniture or decoration in the environment, such as paintings in the boardroom where you are presenting – may compete with you for your audience's attention and should therefore be reduced or removed.

Maximize your contact with your audience by positioning yourself so that you can move and project whilst maintaining visual contact with them. Use your voice to best effect and look and act the part.

Every picture tells a story

Which visual aids to choose

There are few things less convincing, less likely to inform or persuade an audience, than presenters, mumbling head down into their notes, cue cards or scripts. In a large audience, with some expensive technology at your disposal and rehearsal, you could deliver a passable speech by autocue. But this approach doesn't work with smaller audiences in everyday situations.

The purpose of visual aids is twofold – first to provide you with cues and prompts (so that notes can be scrapped), and second to convey your message to your audience visually. Since the majority of people are highly visually oriented and only a smaller proportion auditory, retention is increased dramatically when the message is received through two senses simultaneously.

Your choice of visual medium (multimedia, computer graphics and multimedia back-projection or LCD tablets, 35mm projector, overhead projector, A3/A4 hard copy desk-top presenters) is governed by a variety of factors: the size of room and the audience, environmental factors, availability and accessibility, time to create and produce, cost, level of quality needed and amount of use, to name but a few. Suitability is the most important criterion with speed of production a secondary determinant. Some classic situations are outlined below.

If you have *an audience of less than four*, try to use a desk-top presenter, grouping your audience around a desk where they can all see the A4/A3 visuals. A4 overhead projector acetates can, subject to their colour composition, be used in the presenter. This gives you flexibility if the audience size is larger than you expected.

Don't hand out booklets to the audience and then read through your own copy. You will end up with four or five different presentations underway as they flick through your material at varying speeds. Your focus could be lost, as well as most of what you are saying. Always use a visual device to direct the audience's attention and provide you with an improved level of control. If you can, distribute handouts after your presentation.

If you have *an audience of four or more* use an overhead projector. Quality can be good if you use modern desk-top publishing software and high quality printers to produce them. The type of projector, screen and the degree of direct light can diminish the effect but this method can be used for groups of up to two or three dozen. Lap-top, notebook and desk-top PC screens can be projected on to a larger screen using a powerful overhead projector and an LCD panel or special projection device. However, take hard copies and ordinary acetates just in case of 'technical difficulty'!

If there are *over thirty in your audience*, computer graphics using back-projection equipment or 35mm slides have high definition and can be projected on to a large screen, giving good visibility from a distance. However, because black-out is essential, you will lose eye contact unless you are under a spotlight. A drawback with the 35mm method is that slides cannot easily be amended to include an overnight change in, say, interest rates, figures or legislation. There are cost implications here too. The more flexible and, in the long term, less expensive alternative to 35mm is the use of computer technology, and back projection.

Whichever medium you decide upon there are rules for the preparation of each complete image. Examples of image design formats for both text and graphic visuals are given on pages 87 and 91. These formats have proven to be effective both for the presenter as a prompting device and for the audience as a visualization of content.

Formatting your visual aids

Your visuals should be designed primarily for you as a prompt. If they don't prompt you and you can't deliver from them, the chances of them proving useful to the audience are slim indeed. Follow the guidelines below and make life easier for yourself (and your audience).

1 **Title** your slide and save your audience the trouble of trying to work out what the image is all about. All you want to do is introduce it at this stage and identify what you will be talking about.

2 **Separate** the individual points on your slide by using bullets, letters or numbers.

   • Numbers are used to indicate a priority order or a hierarchy of importance with the most important point being number one.

   • Letters indicate a sequence – step a) is followed by step b) and so on. They can also be used when presenting options. Separating your points in this way is particularly effective when your visual contains diagramatic information. The need to point, wave at or otherwise indicate specific parts of the graphic is removed if you label them appropriately and cross-reference them to each bullet point.

   • If there is neither hierarchy nor sequence, use plain bullets. Squares, triangles, dots or asterisks will indicate whether the six lines on your visual are three pairs, two sets of three or some other combination.

3 Always use **upper and lower case text**, never purely capitals. This makes the slide easier to read. People read by pattern recognition, identifying the shapes that words make – the dots on the 'i's, the tail of the 'y's and the 'g's or the cross of the 't's. Block capitals only offer a series of rectangles of varying lengths. It is also the visual equivalent of shouting at your audience!

4 **Use colour** sparingly, preferably using white or yellow text on a blue background or, if necessary, blue, black or green on a paler or clear background. Never use red for text as it tends to fade into the slide rather than stand out. Use red to underline, high-

light or block around. Never place red and green together in charts, as they are the two colours that colour-blind people usually find hard to differentiate.

5 Remember the **six-by-six rule**. Six words per line (give or take the odd preposition) is just right. Six lines per slide, excluding title and 'strap line' is the maximum. Any more and the slide becomes cluttered, any less and you may have to commit too much to memory. If you rely on memory you risk drying up or resorting to ad-lib – either will cause you real problems. Avoid using bullet point items of only one or two words; they are confusing for your audience, give an insufficient prompt and, if given as hard copy will not be sufficient to remind your audience of your points at a later date. Each bullet point must make an intelligible statement.

6 Finally, each slide needs a **strap line**, to give your audience the message: this is the overall point of the visual that you want them to remember. If they remember this key point they are more likely to remember some of the things you have just said on this subject. The strap line encapsulates all you want to convey with that particular visual – it's the reason you put the slide up in the first place.

Design your visuals in 'landscape' (that is, horizontal) format which gives you a more symmetrical working area. Using the vertical (portrait) format may entail spreading the bullet point items over two lines. The portrait format suits written documents not visual aids.

Software design gives rise to a particular problem when using **graphics**. In translating figures into a pie-chart or graph, the software will use the whole of the image area for display. While it may be said that every picture tells a story no matter how good the graphic, the story may not be that clear. For example, in a pie-chart, which is the significant piece – the largest or the smallest? In a graph is it the peaks or the troughs? Your audience needs more help. Our graphic format shown in Figure 6.2 (page 89) includes the bullet points to remove ambiguity or confusion and the strap line to convey the overall message. Conversely, charts that work well in publications often give excessive detail. You need to simplify this in a visual aid to illustrate a less cluttered image of the particular trend. Designing your visuals using our graphic format acts as a discipline and prevents you having to undergo a mid-presentation memory test. Your audience will be presented with a more complete image – the visual image, its identity, your translation of the image and the overall message.

Aim to speak with each visual format for one and a half to two minutes. This avoids a rapid succession of slide changes during your presentation, which can be confusing and unsettling for your audience.

If you present with a particular slide for more than two minutes, consider breaking the material down into two slides.

Remember the two essential functions of your visuals:

- **to give you your cues and prompts**, and
- **to let your audience see what you're saying as they hear you say it**.

The importance of the question-and-answer session

Given the choice most presenters prefer the formal one-way presentation and loathe the question-and-answer session. There are, however, some presenters who prefer the conversation style of question and answer with smaller audiences.

Our original research found that, in the hour allocated at a 'beauty parade' or new business pitch, most presenting teams opted for a 35–45 minute pitch leaving the remaining 15 minutes for the question-and-answer session. When the audiences were asked what they wanted they responded with precisely the opposite. They preferred 15 minutes of crisp, cogent argument followed by 45 minutes of in-depth questioning. Understandably, many presenters were uncomfortable with this because they didn't think they could package their message effectively in such a short space of time, and, more importantly, they didn't relish the thought of spending all that subsequent time fending off questions. The short one-way, longer two-way approach, however, is indeed the one that you should adopt. It meets the client requirements and avoids dilution of your message in an overlong presentation. There are also two other important reasons for preferring this strategy.

First, the general passive adult attention span – the average time that an audience can remain attentive to a presenter – in the UK is about 13 minutes. Of course, there are variations in individual interest level and powers of concentration but usually, beyond that time, people become increasingly selective about what they hear and are therefore likely to take less and less in. If you speak for more than 13 minutes your audience could easily be switching off at a crucial moment in your pitch. Bearing this in mind, at every 'beauty parade', conference or product launch for which we've helped clients prepare, the main messages (not necessarily all the information) have always been packaged within a 15-minute horizon. Your presentation can, and *should*, always be short.

The second reason for keeping the balance short on input and long on question-and-answer concerns the way that people respond to new ideas, new information and, most importantly, a decision. There are many illustrations of this response but perhaps the most evident is the growth in the 'change management' industry. This area of business consulting depends for its momentum on the fact that faced with new ideas or a concept that conflicts with the way they see the world, most people will want to evaluate negatively or appraise critically the suggestion or proposal before they accept it. They will want to satisfy themselves that there's nothing wrong with it first. You may well have had this experience yourself. When you're presenting to clients and colleagues, and you're telling them things that they already agree with, you should have few problems. However, if you present them with a new product or service or a new way of doing things then, in most cases, their response will be to evaluate negatively, appraise critically, even test destructively the new concepts to satisfy themselves that there is nothing wrong with them. Don't take it personally but minimize the problem. The longer you spend presenting your new ideas and new concepts, the more negative evaluation you will stimulate. You will therefore encounter a wider 'evaluation gap' and will also have correspondingly less time to identify and close that gap. Changing to a shorter presentation and a longer question-and-answer session gives the audience less to critically appraise and to take issue with, and gives you more time in the ensuing session – the interactive part – to deal with any negative evaluation. (One positive by-product of this negative evaluation effect is in 'beauty parades' where the incumbent managers or providers are usually in a stronger position than their competitors – assuming the replace decision has not finally been taken – better the devil you know than the one you don't!)

So, while the first reason for a short input concerns how much of what you say is taken in by your audience, the second reason concerns how much is actually *accepted*. The way you respond to questions, then, is the key to gaining acceptance and agreement from the audience. If the one-way presentation is concerned with making your messages clear, the two-way session is about resolving any negative evaluation of them, manifested in the questions asked.

Strategies for handling questions

In handling questions the presenter typically takes a question from the audience, provides an answer, then takes the next question and so on. As a strategy this leaves much to be desired, not least because all of the direction and control is coming from the audience. In addition, the answers are supplying yet more information which is subject to further critical appraisal. Moreover, there is no way of knowing whether the answers are improving matters, making them worse or having no effect at all. In other words, this stategy doesn't tell you whether you're winning or losing.

Another approach, one favoured by trainers and school-teachers, is to throw the question back to the audience – the 'Well, what do you think?' technique. This is dangerous. The questioner is unsatisfied and may even feel threatened by the risk of exposure, and the audience may conclude that you are being evasive. You can use this approach to clarify the original question or to gain a little thinking time but, once the question is clarified, you must answer it.

The correct strategy – the only one which allows you to retain some control and successfully respond – depends on a crucial realization – *you are not there simply to provide answers to questions*. Your goal is much more important than that – it is to identify the nature of the evaluation gap and close it. This is your primary role in the question-and-answer session.

The way to deal with questions is to take the question from the audience, provide a short answer then put a question back to the questioner to find out if your answer is satisfactory. Keeping the answer short is critical. Lengthy answers usually introduce new material which will be subjected to yet more negative evaluation. They can also lead you into saying something that you regret – and we've all done that. But, most importantly, when questioners in the audience were asked what they thought of the long answers they received, they almost unanimously responded that the question had been answered in the first sentence and that the rest added little value. Long answers are fraught with risks and have very little positive potential. If your initial short response is unsatisfactory, you can always add to it. You cannot, however, retract four and a half minutes of your dangerous 'surplus-to-requirements' response once you've given it.

How to assess if your answer has closed the gap

Always assume that each question is the result of negative evaluation – the gap between where the questioner (and the audience) is and where you would like them to be. The test-back question is designed to discover whether your answer has resolved that negative evaluation and whether the gap is closed?

A full understanding of the nature of the gap can be obtained by considering the four basic reasons why people ask questions:

1 **Information**. They are looking for something that was not mentioned or not covered in sufficient detail in your presentation – there's an information gap.
2 **Clarification**. Something you said was not clear – there's a gap in their understanding.
3 **Doubt/concern**. They doubt what you're saying or are concerned about an aspect of it – there's a credibility gap.
4 **Test**. They wish to test you, your company, your products or services in a pass/fail way. The success of your pitch may depend entirely on knowing the correct answer here.

Listening to the language of the question usually reveals the nature of the gap. Providing information will usually close the first gap, but with 'clarification' the questioner is saying that they have the information but don't understand it. Further explanation is needed to close the gap. In 'doubt/concern' the questioner has the information and they understand it – they just don't believe it. The gap is getting *wider*. With the test question you have to get through the 'gate' and pass.

So, if it's an information question all you have to do is provide the information to close the gap, and then ask:

- 'Does that answer your question?'
- 'Is that OK?'
- 'Are you happy with that?'

Once you receive acknowledgement that the gap is closed, you may move on to the next question.

With a clarification question using the above test-back questions may not work since they carry the risk that the questioner may well confirm their satisfaction while privately thinking 'I'm still as confused as ever'. So you need to be more specific, asking them:

- 'Is that now clear?'
- 'Does that clarify that?'
- 'Does that clear it up for you?'
- 'Do you understand that?'
- 'Can you see what we're driving at?'

If the language of the question implies some doubt then the questioner has not accepted your argument. So having answered, it's no good asking 'Does that answer your question?'. The response could be 'Yes, thank you' whilst really thinking 'I'm more against it now than I was when I started'. You need a much stronger affirmation:

- 'Does that allay your fears about . . . ?'
- 'Does that resolve any concerns you have about this?'

- 'Has that removed your doubts?'
- 'Are you convinced?'

In this way you seek a much clearer affirmation, and you make it much more difficult for the questioner to say 'yes' but mean 'no' without actually lying (and you can usually detect the lie in the tone of their response).

The easiest way to pass a test is to know the answer. The technique for dealing with the test question differs slightly from the others. If you are asked: 'Do you invest in . . . [a country, sector or company with a bad public image]?' or 'Do you use futures?' remain neutral and, before you answer, question back by asking:

- 'Do I take it you have some strong feelings about . . . ?' or
- 'Do you yourself have any view about how you would like to see futures operate in your portfolio?'

Of course there is always the risk that they will respond negatively – 'It's not my view I'm interested in, it's yours. Please just answer the question!' – but this is rare, and the only way you can possibly pass the test (even if only indirectly) is by gaining information that enables you to condition your response:

- 'We share your sentiments about . . . entirely, but many of our clients feel that pressure will eventually bring about significant changes and want to see stronger links, so for these clients we do make the investments.'
- 'While some of our clients feel that futures offer the possibility of significant gain for an acceptable level of risk, we can see that this may not be appropriate for you.'

Conditioning your reply by finding out what the questioner thinks is your first step in answering a test question. Then test back by asking:

- 'Does that seem an unreasonable approach?'
- 'Would you share our views on this?'
- 'Can you go along with us on that?'

Using the question-and-answer technique

The question-and-answer technique is based on a simple categorization system. Whether the question is about information, clarification, doubt or a test, the approach still involves giving a short answer then testing back. Many presenters have difficulty with this, usually because they make their answers too long. They confuse quantity with quality, becoming embroiled in the content of the answer and losing sight of their purpose which is to flush out the negative evaluation and close the evaluation gap.

Remember this three-stage process:

1 Listen carefully to the language of the question – pause before answering.
2 Keep your answer short.
3 Cultivate the automatic habit of asking a question – any question – for affirmation, such as 'OK with that?'. Once you've developed this habit, refine the technique into a more sophisticated, conversational approach which is to listen to the language of the question and reflect this back on the questioner. For example, in response to 'I still can't see why this is the approach to take – can you restate your case?' give your answer and then test back with 'Now can you see why this is the approach to take?'.

Additional techniques

Your use of the question/answer/test-back formula will be complemented by the following techniques which address the most common situations.

No questions

This is a common problem, particularly with larger groups where no one likes to be first. The strategy here is to 'prime the pump' by having a few self-imposed questions prepared. Preface them with 'We are sometimes asked . . .'.

There may be cultural differences to consider. For example, if you ask an Asian audience 'Are there any questions?' this could be misinterpreted as 'Is there anything you have failed to understand?'. Instead, treat your short presentation as an appreciation and ask which areas they would now like you to expand on in more detail. However, this approach may still fail to produce questions in certain oriental cultures where questioning the presenter would be considered impolite. In these circumstances be prepared to pose and answer all of the questions yourself. Don't be tempted to structure a full hour of presentation; keep the initial presentation short to keep the messages clear.

You don't know the answer

Never say 'I don't know'. This is not the occasion for public confessions of ignorance. Use a euphemism: 'I need to gather more information to give a complete answer' or 'I don't have that information to hand'. Offer to supply the questioner with the answer by a certain time (and make sure you do so).

Persistent questions

Sometimes you may encounter a questioner who just won't let go. The technique here is, after several related questions, to use the rest of the audience (often the questioner's colleagues) and to take it 'off line'. Ask them if they want to go into this level of detail, or whether you and the questioner should discuss this on an individual basis. If they say that they do want to hear your answers, you will know that the whole group shares this interest. If, as often happens, they say they don't want to pursue this then they have made the decision and you can move on, postponing your discussion until after the question-and-answer session.

Ritual prefacing

When answering questions avoid prefacing your response with phrases such as these:

- 'I'm glad you asked that.'
- 'That's an interesting question.'
- 'That's a good question.'

Apart from the fact that such phrases patronize your audience (they don't appreciate scores for the value of their questions), any other questioner who doesn't receive this type of initial response may feel slighted.

Remain neutral – don't preface your answer with such patronizing comments.

Team questions

Each member should answer on their individual subject areas which are allocated in advance. Exceptions to these areas should be dealt with by the team leader. Never volunteer additional information to supplement another member's answers because it devalues them. Only contribute if invited. The team leader is responsible for asking the test-back questions. Without this team management the capacity for your team to look as if they 'first met in the taxi' is substantial – therefore plan thoroughly.

The all-important summary

The final technique to help you ensure success is to summarize briefly your principal messages again at the end of the question-and-answer session. The final thing your audience should hear are the things you want them to remember – your key messages, not your response to the last question, which might have been a particularly difficult one. Remember the presentation lasted about 15 minutes, the question-and-answer session up to 45 minutes, and your messages may have been lost. You must refresh everyone's memory before you close.

The question-and-answer session is where presentations are won or lost. Adopting the approach described here is crucial to your success.